1955

IN SPORT

1955
IN SPORT
A YEAR LIKE NONE OTHER

Introduction by DAVE ANDERSON

SPORT CLASSIC BOOKS

Published in the United States of America by Sport Media
    Publishing Inc., Wilmington, Delaware, and
    simultaneously in Canada.

For information about permission to reproduce selections
    from this book, please write to:
    Permissions
    Sport Media Publishing, Inc.,
    21 Carlaw Ave.,
    Toronto, Ontario, Canada, M4M 2R6
    www.sportclassicbooks.com

Cover design: Paul Hodgson / pHd
Cover Photograph: The SPORT Collection

Interior design: Greg Oliver
This book is set in AGaramond, 11/12.5 point.

ISBN: 1-894963-35-0

Library of Congress Control Number: 2004106887

Printed in Canada

Dedication

To some of the greats who left us in 1955: former world heavyweight boxing champion Tommy Burns (May 10); F1 driver Alberto Ascari (May 26); Indy 500 driver Wild Bill Vukovich (May 31); baseball player and manager Clark Griffith (Oct. 27); and two baseball immortals, Cy Young (Nov. 4) and Honus Wagner (Dec. 6).

Note From The Publisher

The articles from *SPORT* included in this book are reprinted exactly as they originally appeared in the magazine. Many words and phrases commonplace in the middle years of the 20th century sound peculiar or, in the occasional instance, perhaps even offensive today. However, it was determined that altering the original language would diminish the accuracy and, ultimately, value of the strong historical context contained in the articles, and should therefore be avoided.

Contents

BOB
COUSY

TONY
TRABERT

HOWARD
CASSADY

ARNOLD
SOWELL

CARY
MIDDLECOFF

PAT
MCCORMICK

HARLON
HILL

WALTER
ALSTON

ROY
CAMPANELLA

ROCKY
MARCIANO

NASHUA

ROCKET
RICHARD

BILL
RUSSELL

SPORT TOP PERFORMERS OF 1955

A Year Like
None Other

By Dave Anderson

YOU DIDN'T HAVE to be there.

Looking back now, you didn't have to be around sports in 1955 to appreciate how important some people were then, or how even more important they would still be now: Jackie Robinson and the Brooklyn Dodgers, Willie Mays, Mickey Mantle, Eddie Mathews, Bill Russell, Wilt Chamberlain, Doak Walker, Rocky Marciano, Sugar Ray Robinson, the Montreal Canadiens, Arnold Palmer, Pancho Gonzalez and Bill Vukovich.

You didn't have to be there, but I was.

When the Dodgers won the 1955 World Series on Johnny Podres' 2-0 shutout of the Yankees in the seventh game, I was there for the New York *Journal-American* after having covered the Dodgers for the Brooklyn *Eagle* in 1953 and 1954. Those two newspapers don't exist now. Neither, of course, do the Brooklyn Dodgers. After the 1957 season, their owner, Walter O'Malley, absconded with the franchise to Los Angeles, never to return. Oldtimers in Brooklyn still curse O'Malley, and will until they die.

You can't blame them. Without the Dodgers, Brooklyn has never been the same.

Then again, baseball has never been the same. With the Dodgers in Los Angeles and the New York Giants moving to San Francisco, the big leagues stretched from coast to coast at a time when baseball was *the* sport. Pro football was just starting to catch on. College football was important, but scattered. Pro basketball was still growing. College basketball was trying to recover from a point-shaving scandal. Boxing was big, but mostly in New York and Chicago. Hockey had only six teams. Golf and tennis were seldom on television.

Only a decade after the end of World War II, the world was different in 1955 than it is now. Much different.

Dwight D. Eisenhower, the Army general who organized the D-Day invasion of Normandy in World War II, was the President who would establish the Interstate highway system. But the Berlin Wall was up and the Cold War was on. The Soviet Union was developing a space program that would put Sputnik in orbit. Fidel Castro was plotting his communist takeover of Cuba. Television sets were in black and white. Jet airliners were about to replace propeller-driven planes but nobody knew what computers or cellphones were.

Sports were different too.

Major-league baseball wasn't even thinking of expanding to Houston, Montreal, Anaheim and Toronto, or creating the New York Mets. Pro football had yet to assemble the American Football League. In pro basketball, the Lakers represented Minneapolis; other franchises were in Rochester, Syracuse, Fort Wayne and St. Louis. The National Hockey League had two teams in the Northeast (New York Rangers, Boston Bruins), two in the Midwest (Detroit Red Wings, Chicago Blackhawks), and two in Canada (Montreal Canadiens, Toronto Maple Leafs).

Boxing was a Friday night staple, especially in bars that had a television set for all those who didn't. Golf and tennis weren't much more than a rumor. Auto racing was the Indianapolis 500. The Olympics were basically a track meet in Europe, although Melbourne, Australia, was awaiting the 1956 Summer Games.

Not until 1956 did CBS televise some regular-season pro football games to selected markets across the nation. Cable television didn't exist. Major-league baseball was mostly seen in local markets. Quick sports-news radio shows were heard and every so often a station experimented with what is now considered a sports talk show, but there were no TV panel sports shows.

To know anything about sports in 1955 you had to listen to radio play-by-play of whatever local game you were interested in, then read the newspapers the next day or *The Sporting News*, a weekly that just covered baseball.

You also had to read *SPORT* magazine.

In August of 1946, I remember being on vacation with my parents in Vermont when I glanced at a magazine rack in a country store and noticed the first issue of *SPORT* magazine. On the cover, Joe DiMaggio, in his Yankee pinstriped uniform, had his arm around Joe, Jr., who was wearing a little Yankee cap. As I remember, it cost 25 cents. By the time I fell asleep that night, I had read every story in it. And every month after that, I waited for it to arrive at my neighborhood candy store in the Bay Ridge section of Brooklyn, not far from where the Verrazano Bridge is now. In those years, candy stores sold newspapers, magazines, stationery supplies and most of them had a soda fountain where you could get an egg cream (chocolate syrup, milk and seltzer).

And after the first editions of the *Daily News* (2 cents) and the *Daily Mirror* (2 cents) arrived around 8 o'clock at night, you stood on the street corner and debated why the Dodgers had won or lost.

Unlike almost everybody else in Brooklyn, I was not a devoted Dodger fan. I considered myself a baseball fan. The game meant more to me any one team, but I'll confess: when the St. Louis Cardinals overtook the Dodgers for the 1942 National League pennant, I liked their red-trimmed uniforms with the two cardinals perched on a bat, but mostly I liked Stan Musial. Stan the Man was my man. He even kept me in pocket money.

Whenever the Cardinals were coming into Ebbets Field for a four-game weekend series with the Dodgers—Friday night, Saturday afternoon, Sunday doubleheader—I would bet the guys I hung out with on the corner of Third Avenue and 72nd St. that Musial would get at least six hits in the four games. Each bet was maybe a quarter. That may not sound like much but at the time 25 cents was enough to go to the movies at Loew's Bay Ridge theater. And thanks to Stan the Man, I almost always collected a few quarters.

Years later, Stan laughed when I told him how sometimes he was worth as much as $2 to me whenever the Cardinals had a weekend series at Ebbets Field.

In those years right after the War, baseball was really America's game, its only game, and mostly an afternoon game. During my summer vacations from Xavier High School in Manhattan, I worked as a copyboy in the sports department of the New York *Sun*. I tore the play-by-play copy of the afternoon games off the Associated Press machine, handed it to an editor who marked it up with a heavy black pencil, then I put it in a pneumatic tube that whooshed it to the composing room. Every few hours, I hurried down to the press room and brought up a dozen copies of the latest edition, literally hot off the presses.

My first summer there, 1945, I remember seeing two big black headlines on the front page, one with "Atom Bomb" in it, the other celebrating Japan's surrender.

I had been promised a job as a reporter on the *Sun* when I graduated from Holy Cross College in 1951, but midway through my junior year the *Sun* folded. Luckily, the Brooklyn *Eagle* had an opening for a clerk in its sports department. I was hired for $40 a week. Even luckier, in 1952 I occasionally covered some of the Yankees' and the Giants' home games, then early in the 1953 season the Dodgers' beat writer, elderly Harold C. Burr, broke his hip in a fall in a Cincinnati hotel. Covering the Dodgers along with several older and more experienced writers from the other New York newspapers, I learned how to do the job in self-defense. I mostly kept my mouth shut and my ears open as the Dodgers won the pennant in 1953, but lost the World Series to the Yankees (again), then finished second to the Giants in 1954. Early in 1955 my wife Maureen and I had our suitcases packed to go to spring training with our first son, five-month-old Stephen, when the *Eagle* reporters went on strike for higher pay. Seven weeks later, after the publisher's strike insurance expired, he folded the *Eagle*.

Two days later, the *Journal-American* hired me. That's how I happened to be covering the 1955 World Series, the only Series the Dodgers ever won while representing Brooklyn.

Over the years at the *Journal-American*, I covered baseball, pro football, hockey, tennis and boxing. When the *Journal-American* merged with the *World-Telegram & Sun* and the *Herald-Tribune* into the *World Journal Tribune* that disappeared after nine months, I moved to *The New York Times* to cover baseball, pro and college football, pro and college basketball, boxing, hockey and tennis. I've been a columnist there since 1971.

But to me, my real claim to fame is that I was the last sportswriter to cover the Brooklyn Dodgers for the Brooklyn *Eagle*, especially in the years when Jackie Robinson played.

Jackie Robinson was the best baseball player I've ever seen because he could win a game so many different ways—with a single or a home run, with an inning-ending catch, with a stolen base or rattling the pitcher into a balk, or sometimes with his competitive fire that inspired his teammates.

I've always believed that Robinson's popularity was the

JACKIE ROBINSON

reason the Dodgers traded him to the New York Giants after the 1956 season, the deal that prompted his retirement. Walter O'Malley had always resented Robinson's admiration for Branch Rickey, the previous Dodger owner who had signed Robinson in 1945, breaking the color line that had existed among the other 15 major-league club owners for so long.

O'Malley knew that when and if the franchise moved to Los Angeles that Robinson, who grew up in nearby Pasadena, would emerge someday as a popular choice to be the Dodgers manager. By trading Robinson to the Giants, O'Malley made sure that he would never need to consider Robinson as a manager in Los Angeles.

Robinson faded into retirement rather than report to the hated Giants—that's how seriously some players took a rivalry in those years before the players' union. Bobby

Thomson, who hit the home run for the Giants that won the 1951 pennant in a playoff with the Dodgers, told me years later that whenever the Giants walked through Ebbets Field's common runway from the dugouts to their respective clubhouses, he never even looked at or spoke to any of the Dodgers.

"Except Gil Hodges," Thomson said. "I'd say hello to Gil Hodges."

When Willie Mays crumpled to the base of the left-centerfield wall in Ebbets Field after making a sensational catch, his Giants teammates and manager Leo Durocher rushed out there. So did Jackie Robinson.

"I thought Jackie wanted to see if I was all right," Mays has often said, "but he just wanted to make sure the ball was still in my glove."

That was baseball in those years, but Mays' emergence as arguably its brightest star couldn't prevent the Giants from abandoning the Polo Grounds and moving to San Francisco. Two teams on the West Coast simplified the other six National League teams' travel plans. But the Yankees' success in winning six World Series from 1947 to 1953 didn't stop Yankee Stadium fans from brutally booing Mickey Mantle during the 1955 season. Why? For all his rave notices, he hadn't been able to make them forget Joe DiMaggio.

Perhaps coincidentally, the Mick erupted in 1956 as a Triple Crown winner—leading the American League in batting (.353), home runs (52) and runs batted in (130). That silenced the boo birds.

Another home-run hitter, Eddie Mathews, had helped to put Milwaukee on the major-league map. In the first migration of baseball franchises westward, the Braves had moved there from Boston in 1953 and Mathews gave the

Milwaukee fans, who led the majors in attendance, somebody to cheer. When the Braves won the 1957 World Series from the Yankees and won the NL pennant in 1958 before losing the Series to the Yankees, Mathews and Hank Aaron were their most formidable hitters. Aaron, of course, would go on to hit a record 755 homers, but in 1955, after having slugged 47 homers in 1953 and 40 in 1954, Eddie Mathews was the man in Milwaukee.

Red Auerbach is a pro basketball icon for having had a direct part as coach and/or general manager in molding the Boston Celtics dynasty: 16 championships, including 9 in 11 seasons. But in 1955 when the Celtics were struggling, he knew he needed a "good big fellow to get me the ball." He tried to get a Philadelphia schoolboy named Wilt Chamberlain to go to Harvard so the Celtics could take him in the territorial draft that existed then. Chamberlain would enroll at the University of Kansas, but a year later Auerbach would get the "good big fellow" he needed: Bill Russell.

In the mid-'50s, pro football had not yet gripped America; that would happen in the 1958 NFL championship game when Johnny Unitas led the Baltimore Colts to a 23-17 victory over the New York Giants in sudden-death overtime. But in 1955, Doak Walker played his last season for the Detroit Lions after having helped them win two NFL title games against the Cleveland Browns. But whatever he did for the Lions was merely an extension of the legend he created as a Southern Methodist running back who won the 1948 Heisman Trophy.

Just as college football was big in 1955, so was boxing—especially Rocky Marciano, the only world heavyweight champion to retire undefeated: 49-0 with 43 knockouts. Years later Larry Holmes got to 48-0, but lost his 49th fight to Michael Spinks. For all the commotion and devotion that Muhammad Ali generated, he lost now and then. George Foreman lost. Joe Frazier lost. Mike Tyson lost. Joe Louis lost. Jack Dempsey lost. Jack Johnson lost. John L. Sullivan lost. But the Rock never lost. He would die in a 1969 crash of a small plane.

But for all of Marciano's popularity in 1955, Sugar Ray Robinson represented boxing's comeback story while enhancing the crown that still fits him half a century later—pound for pound, the best boxer in history. With his Harlem business enterprises sabotaged by distrustful employees, the man born Walker Smith had to resume boxing in order to earn enough money to pay his bills

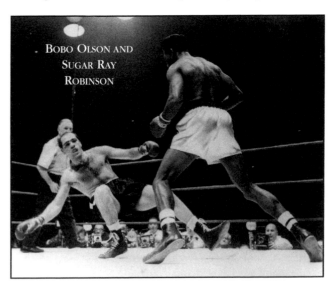

BOBO OLSON AND SUGAR RAY ROBINSON

and restore his lifestyle. After several shaky fights, he not only regained the world middleweight championship with a second-round knockout of Carl (Bobo) Olson, then knocked out Olson in the fourth round of a rematch. He went on to hold the middleweight title a record five times.

In hockey, the Stanley Cup has resided recently in some strange locales—under Tampa Bay's palm trees or alongside the New Jersey Turnpike. But in 1955, the Cup had never traveled very far in the six-team National Hockey League, mostly to Montreal, Toronto or Detroit. But when the Montreal Canadiens went to training camp that year under a new coach, Hector (Toe) Blake, they were assembling the team that would keep the Cup for a record five consecutive years (1956-1960) in the nation of its origin, Canada.

Before or since, hockey never had a team like those Canadiens. Their power play was so dominating, it changed the rules. With Maurice Richard at right wing, Jean Beliveau at center, Bert Olmstead at left wing, Doug Harvey and Boom-Boom Geoffrion on the points, the Canadiens often scored two, or occasionally three, goals during an opposing player's two-minute penalty, prompting the National Hockey League to decide that when any team's power play scored, the penalized player could immediately return to the ice.

Auto racing is mostly NASCAR now, but in 1955 the Daytona 500 didn't even exist; it wasn't run until 1959. In what was known in 1955 as stock-car's Grand National Championship, Tim Flock, in a Chrysler, was the leading driver but the prize money was so paltry his earnings that year were a measly $33,750—that wouldn't buy his fuel today. In auto racing back then, the money and the acclaim centered on the Indianapolis 500, especially in the weeks leading up to the 1955 race after Bill Vukovich, in a Fuel-Injection Special, had won there in both 1953 and 1954. At the time only two other drivers, Wilbur Shaw and Mauri Rose, had won back-to-back Indy 500s.

In 1955, golf was also developing its own power play in the person and the personality of Arnold Palmer, the ruggedly handsome son of a Latrobe, Pa. club pro, who was in his first season on the PGA Tour after having been the 1954 United States Amateur champion. Over the next decade as golf's first television star he would be the first four-time winner of the Masters, the winner of the 1960 United States Open with a come-from-behind final-round 65 that put the word "charge" in golf's vocabulary, and a two-time winner of the British Open. Half a century later, when some people think of golf, they still think first of Arnold Palmer.

While golf soon would begin to boom after Palmer's arrival, tennis had an identity problem. Its best player, Richard (Pancho) Gonzalez, who grew up on the cement public courts of Los Angeles, might as well have been in hiding. Thirteen years before the tennis solons approved open tournaments, allowing pros to compete against amateurs on the hallowed courts of Wimbledon and the United States, Australian and French championships, Gonzalez was a champion without a court.

After winning the U.S. National singles at Forest Hills in both 1948 and 1949, Gonzalez had turned pro in order to cash in on his ability, as most amateur champions did then. But pro tennis was a long and lonely tour of one-night stands, the new challenger against the old champion in a traveling one-ring circus.

Gonzalez soon reigned, so much so that by 1955 he not only had conquered all his foes, no new amateur champion dared to turn pro and challenge him. Suddenly there was no pro tour in 1955. The best tennis player in the world had nobody to play and nowhere to go. The next year he did, routing Tony Trabert, the 1954 and 1955 U.S. champion, and later Ken Rosewall, the little Australian who had won the 1956 U.S. title. The following year, he dispatched Lew Hoad, the blond Australian who had won Wimbledon in 1956 and 1957.

Pro tennis at least was alive again. So was Gonzalez, who endured to enjoy the stage of open competition at Wimbledon and Forest Hills. As late as 1970 he opened a tournament at Madison Square Garden with an epic five-set victory over Rod Laver, who the year before had completed the first open grand slam by winning the Australian, French, Wimbledon and U.S. singles titles.

Of all the 1955 personalities in this book, Pancho Gonzalez is the least remembered, the least appreciated because his sport betrayed him. Tennis didn't wake up to the importance of allowing pros to compete on the biggest and best stages of its most prestigious tournaments until he was well past his prime. All the others in this book always had access to the biggest and best stages in their sport. Some needed time to get there, but eventually, they were center stage. And now they're center stage again in this book.

The Dodgers Strain For A Championship

The 1955 Brooklyn Dodgers may not be the greatest base-ball team in history, but even today it is difficult to name a team that is more loved. They entered 1955 as a seven-time winner of the National League pennant—and seven-time World Series loser, including five defeats between 1941 and 1953 to the New York Yankees. But 1955 was Brooklyn's year. These were the Dodgers of Roy Campanella, Duke Snider, Don Newcombe, Gil Hodges, Jackie Robinson, Pee Wee Reese, Carl Furillo, and Johnny Podres. As recounted here by Frank Graham, they bolted to the fastest start in baseball history, coasted to the pennant and defeated the hated Yankees in an electric seven-game Series. But that was Brooklyn's lone Series championship. Owner Walter O'Malley moved the franchise—hijacked it, many still say—to Los Angeles in 1958, leaving Brooklynites, most of whom never forgave O'Malley, to live off the memories of one glorious summer.

BY FRANK GRAHAM
FEBRUARY 1956

THE RECORD IS that the Dodgers won the National League pennant last year by 13-1/2 games, which makes it appear that they won it in a romp. As a matter of fact, they did. They got off on what the race trackers call "the Bill

1

Daly," meaning on the front end, and they never were headed. Yet, along the way, there were some injuries, some pulling and hauling among them, some huffing and puffing and a snarl here and there, and at such times the opposing clubs were less of a bother to them than they were themselves.

The one who calmed them down or brought them up short when danger threatened, however remotely, was Walter Alston. The year before, Alston had been hired to beat the Yankees in the World Series. When he didn't, more than one of his critics suggested to club president Walter O'Malley that he be sent back to the bushes, whence Walter had whistled him up when Charlie Dressen wrote himself out of the big-league action in a four-page letter. Instead, O'Malley, who had signed Alston for only one year, signed him for another. So early last spring, he was at Vero Beach where, in keeping with the axiom that life copies art, the Dodgers were working on a real life version of Abbott and Costello's famous baseball routine. Had you wandered into the camp in quest of at least a tentative lineup of the squad for the start of the 1955 season, you would have come off with, roughly, this:

"Who's on first?"

"Hodges, of course. That is, if he doesn't play left field."

"If Hodges doesn't play left field, who will?"

"Robinson. Although Robinson may play third base."

"Who's at shortstop?"

"Reese, naturally. Unless he plays third base—or second."

"Second? What about Gilliam?"

"Oh, he won't be around long. He's on the block."

"Well, if Hodges goes to left field . . . ."

"Then Robinson will play first base."

"But I thought if Robinson didn't go to left field, he'd play third base."

"Hoak could play third base."

"And if Reese, who could play shortstop or third base, goes to second, who'll play shortstop?"

"Maybe Zimmer."

"Well, now that the infield has been settled, how about Campanella?"

"How about him? He says his hand is all right. But who knows?"

"And Newcombe?"

"Who knows about him, either? He talks big. He always talks big."

"Erskine . . . Loes . . . Spooner . . . Meyer . . . the rest of the pitchers. How about them?"

"Who knows?"

"Is there anybody on the ball club anybody knows anything about?"

"Oh, sure. The Duke will be in center field and Furillo in right."

Funny? It wasn't funny to Alston. Neither were his press conferences, at which the reporters, eager to get as clear a picture of the situation as they could for presentation to their readers, hammered him with questions he could not answer. How could he? At that point, he was unsure of some of his players because they were unsure of themselves. He had to see what they could do before he could make any commitments.

The relationship between himself and Robinson, if not precisely strained, was by no means cordial. He was waiting for Robinson to get in shape before passing judgment on him and thought talking to him about it unnecessary. Robinson didn't talk to him but he did talk to the reporters. He said he didn't know where he was going to play or even whether or not he would be traded. He spoke of this being his last season in baseball.

Pee Wee Reese said: "No one has asked me when I'm going to give myself up and take off my uniform but I know that's what a lot of people are wondering. But I feel good and I know I can play this year. I don't know where I will play, though. Walt hasn't said anything to me. I've been meaning to speak to him but I'm a fellow who likes to put things off."

When he got around to asking Walt, Walt said: "Shortstop. Where else?"

So that much was clear, at any rate.

Gil Hodges said: "Naturally, I would prefer to play first base. But I will gladly play anywhere Walt wants me to."

Against the possibility that he might have to use Hodges in left field, Alston had got Frank Kellert from Baltimore for trial at first base. Campanella spoke with restrained enthusiasm about his recovery from the hand injury that had plagued him the year before. Big Newk was very certain of himself but, as far as Alston was concerned, he was strictly on a wait-and-see basis, and Walt wasn't at all sure that what he saw he would like.

Gilliam wandered through the camp like a little lost boy. He had heard that he was about to be traded and believed it. He had good reason to. Vice-president Buzzie Bavasi was trying to make a deal with the Redlegs for Wally Post and a catcher who might be needed in Brooklyn if Campanella's hand hadn't properly healed. Gilliam was marked for just such a trade. It didn't come off but Gilliam couldn't know that it wouldn't. Actually, he didn't know what Buzzie had in mind. All he knew was that something was in the making and that it boded no good for him.

Meanwhile there were two young infielders at whom Alston was looking closely.

"You have been working with Hoak at third base and Zimmer at second base and shortstop," a reporter said to the manager one day. "Does that mean anything?"

"Not necessarily," Alston said.

"Then you have not decided on your infield?"

"No."

Hoak and Zimmer were a confident and tough-minded pair of competitors, despite their inexperience. "I can play third base as good as anybody on this ball club," Hoak said.

"If I ever get in there," Zimmer said, "they'll never get me out."

Their own opinions of themselves obviously topped Alston's, for when the season opened at Ebbets Field on the dark, cold and drizzly afternoon of April 13, with 6,999 fans in the stands, Robinson was on third base and Reese at shortstop. Gilliam, saved from exile to Cincinnati, was on second base and Hodges on first. Snider was in center field, of course, and Furillo in right. The trouble spot in left field was occupied by Sandy Amoros. Campanella, thumping his mitt, talking incessantly to the opposing hitters and, very much himself again, was back of the bat. Carl Erskine was the pitcher. He held the Pirates to seven hits as the Dodgers won, 6-1.

This was the lineup that had emerged from the apparent confusion at Vero Beach, and Alston had reason to be pleased with it. He also had reason to be pleased with the squad as a whole, for no better conditioned club had come out of the South. After that one game at Ebbets Field—the regularly scheduled opening had been postponed—the Dodgers took to the road and, beating the Giants at the Polo Grounds, the Pirates in Pittsburgh and the Phillies in Philadelphia, ran up seven more victories. Returning to Flatbush, they flattened the Phils again for their ninth straight, tying the modern league record for consecutive victories on a season's jump-off.

They were not, however, a particularly happy crew, being puzzled and hurt by the seeming lack of interest on the part of the Brooklyn fans. Their first game back home was a night game that drew only 9,942. The following day, as they knocked out Robin Roberts and belted the Phillies, 14-4 for their tenth in a row, breaking the record, the turnstile count was a paltry 3,874. Robinson, Snider, Amoros and Zimmer—Don was at shortstop because Reese had suffered a groin injury a couple of days before—hit home runs. Zimmer and Furillo each made four hits, Joe Black did a great relief job, taking over from Russ Meyer when the game was tied in the third inning and giving up only two hits the rest of the way. The Dodgers never before had had it so good against Roberts. But in the clubhouse after the game there was little elation. The players were depressed at the apathy of their public.

It was the Duke who, perhaps best of all, put their feelings into printable words. During the game announcer Tex Rickard had said over the public-address system that he would have an important announcement when the game was over. This, it developed, was that souvenirs would be given by the club to all those present who mailed in their ticket stubs. Now, in the clubhouse, the Duke said: "That comes as a big surprise to me. I thought they were going to announce that the franchise would be moved to Los Angeles."

The Giants, moving into Ebbets Field, the following day, won the first game of a three-game series, lost the second and won the third. The Dodgers, who hadn't lost a game up to that time, now had lost a series. This, however, was but a pause in their drive for the flag. As the first invasion of the year by the western clubs got under way, the Dodgers mowed down the Redlegs, the Cubs, the Braves and the Cardinals, running their new count of consecutive victories to seven.

Meanwhile, there had been a few ragged but surprising rumors of dissension among the players. No names were named, no instances cited. But there they were and, on May 5, the day they won the second game of a two-game set with the Cardinals and stretched their lead to seven and a half games, a story broke that brought to light at least one example of the troubles Alston was reported to be having with a group of players who should have given him no trouble at all: Don Newcombe was suspended.

The background of Newcombe's open breach of discipline was this: Although Don was being hailed as the top home-run hitter among pitchers since the days when Babe Ruth was pitching for the Red Sox, his pitching hadn't matched his hitting and for two weeks Alston purposely had bypassed him when it was his turn to start. This so irked Don that when, before this game with the Cardinals, Alston told him to pitch in batting practice, he responded with a flat and angry no.

"Why not?" Alston asked.

"Because," Don said, "I am expecting to pitch in Philadelphia tomorrow and I don't aim to pitch batting practice today."

Alston knew Newcombe from 1946, when Walt was the manager of the Nashua, N.H., club in the Brooklyn farm system and Don was a rookie pitcher. He'd formed then, and retained, a great liking for the big man and this must have come as a shock to him, but he met it firmly.

"Pitch batting practice," he said.

"No," Newcombe said again.

"Take off that uniform," Alston said, "and get out of the park. You're suspended for . . ."

Maybe he couldn't think of the right word. But he completed the sentence with "for disorderly conduct."

This one-man uprising against the authority vested in Alston was short-lived. The following day, summoned to the office for a hearing, Don pleaded guilty, offered no

ROY CAMPANELLA

excuse save his lack of starting assignments, and promised to be amenable from there on. That afternoon, he went to Philadelphia with the Dodgers. That night, as the fifth pitcher in an arduous tussle with the Phillies, he checked their bats until a 12th-inning double by Campanella won the game and increased the Dodgers' lead to eight and a half games as the then second-place Cubs lost to the Redlegs.

In the New York *Daily News*, Dick Young wrote: "Out of 'The Great Newcombe Rebellion,' Walt Alston emerged as the strong man of the Dodgers. Alston's authority has been tested and proven. 'Newk realizes now,' said Veep Buzzie Bavasi, 'that Walt is manager of the club.' So do the rest of the Brooks. It required a showdown that Newcombe forced yesterday."

Bavasi, who had fined Don a day's pay ($104.79, someone figured) said there would be an added penalty, anywhere from $250 to $500. Four days later, as the Dodgers opened a series in Chicago, he pitched a one-hit game. Moreover, he pitched to only 27 men, for Gene Baker, who got the only hit, was thrown out stealing and there were no errors and no bases on balls. After that it seemed unlikely that Newk would have to dig into his poke again—but he did. Bavasi nicked him for $300.

This streak ended the day after Newk's finest game, when the Cubs chased Meyer. But it was only May 11 and the Dodgers were eight and a half games in front. The other clubs quietly girded themselves for the fight for second place. A month later, having pulled themselves together after some shilly-shallying, during which their lead dropped to a mere five and a half games, they were ten and a half in the van. Newcombe, although he frequently had to be relieved, hadn't lost a game and had received credit for ten victories and was hitting close to .400. Snider and Campanella were involved in a home-run race of their own. The original lineup was holding fast. Karl Spooner, the prodigy of 1954, had come on after a slow start and was pulling Newk and Erskine out of trouble when they faltered. Ed Roebuck was another whose part-time pitching was helpful. A pitcher named Johnny Podres was beginning to come through. Another pitcher, this one named Clem Labine, was doing all right, too.

In July, Campanella was forced out with a knee injury and Rube Walker, the almost unknown catcher, filled in for him. When Rube was hurt, Alston reached into the bullpen and came up with the slightly ancient Dixie Howell, who had been signed on only as a pitching coach in the spring but had been so spry at Vero Beach he got a player's contract instead. Then as Campanella came back, Robinson limped out of action with a bad knee, the Duke was knocked out with a virus, Meyer suffered a fracture of his collar bone, and Podres, Erskine and Spooner developed lame arms. Amoros sprained his back chasing flies in left field. Robinson, trying to return to the lineup after a few days' rest, fell on his face when his knee buckled in batting practice.

"This is silly," he said. "Nothing like it ever happened to me before."

Hoak remained at third base. Zimmer played second in place of Gilliam, who went to left field. If not for the 13-game lead they held in early July, the situation might otherwise have seemed alarming. Instead, comforted by their lead, the Dodgers kept right on winning. Even when they came into the Polo Grounds with just four regulars fit to play, they were cool and confident. On July 8, before a sellout of 43,578 people, they overcame an early 6-0 Giant lead by first attacking their old tormentor Sal Maglie as they have rarely attacked him before. They drove him back to the center-field club-house in the fourth inning with a five-run rally and continued to hit his successors freely, until, in the eighth, with the score tied, they had catcher Ray Katt so confused he threw the ball into left field on an attempted pickoff, allowing Zimmer to score the tie-breaking run. They dropped the remaining two games of the weekend series to the Giants, lost their third in a row to the Cardinals back into Brooklyn, before going off on a three-game tear against the Cards and Redlegs.

Alston moved dramatically to bolster his pitching staff. He summoned Roger Craig, who was with the Montreal club in Havana, and Don Bessent from St. Paul. The two of them, flying into Brooklyn from opposite directions, were tossed immediately into a doubleheader with the Redlegs. Craig pitched a three-hitter to win the first game and Bessent, with the help of Roebuck in the ninth, won the second. Although the second-place Braves also won a doubleheader that day, the Dodgers' lead remained at 12-1/2 games. Alston was greatly relieved.

Near the end of the month, when the club was in St. Louis and Robinson still was on the bench, he told Dick Young he felt he might be forced into retirement by a drastic salary cut. "I don't know whether they want me to play any more," he said, "I'd rather quit than argue over money with them. I have a couple of outside offers for next year that, between them, would bring me more than I could expect to make in baseball. More than I'm making now, in fact."

Whatever the reason for the declaration, apart from the fact that Jackie seemed to feel Alston was indifferent about his return to the lineup, it evoked no response from either the manager or the front office and served only to suggest that Jackie had small regard for his employers and even less for Alston. When he did return to the lineup some days later, he was in left field and would alternate between that position and third base for the balance of the season, except when his ailing knee bothered him. Then he would sit out the ball game or, perhaps, see brief action as a pinch-hitter.

August was a lively month for the Dodgers. Newcombe, who had won 18 games, had a rough time trying to win the 19th. Billy Loes, who had not won for a month, looked as though he might never win again and gave it as his opinion that baseball was a lousy game and that the umpires were lousy, too. O'Malley said that if the attendance didn't pick up he would be forced to abandon the obsolete ball park, build a new one in Brooklyn or move the club to another city and that, as an experiment, the Dodgers would play seven scattered games in Jersey City in 1956. A couple of days later, when the Dodgers lost a twi-night doubleheader to the Redlegs and their lead was reduced to 11 games, the fans told them even Jersey City would be too good for them.

This prompted Snider, who had been booed when he made but one hit in nine times at bat in the two games, to yell loudly enough to be quoted in all the papers: "They are the worst fans in baseball! They don't deserve a pennant. That's why we're going to Jersey City next year."

The next night he weighed in with a public, but limited, apology. "I'm sorry, in a way," he said. "I guess I shouldn't have said what I did. There are some good fans in Brooklyn. Some bad ones, too."

That night the good fans cheered him. The bad ones fried his ears.

Still, relentlessly, the Dodgers moved on. Sandy Koufax, 19 years old, Brooklyn born, and discovered for the Dodgers while pitching for the University of Cincinnati (where he had gone on a basketball scholarship) by Cliff Alexander, Alston's brother-in-law, cut the Redlegs down with two hits, shutting them out and fanning 14 of them along the way as the Dodgers won, 7-0. The youth movement in Flatbush progressed as Spooner and Podres hurled the Cardinals back and Newcombe finally managed his 19th victory at the expense of the Braves. Youth? Big Newk? For this one you must look to the footnotes. Newk scored on an assist by Bessent. Spooner shut out the Pirates. So did Koufax. On successive days, that is. Newk won his 20th, beating the Phillies on September 5. The date is important, if not in baseball history, in O'Malley's ledger: On September 5, the largest crowd of the season, 33,451, made the turnstiles spin at Ebbets Field. For that day, at least, Jersey City was forgotten. Newk also hit a home run. It was his seventh of the year.

The crowd was there to bid farewell to the Dodgers until World Series time, for they were about to leave on their last swing of the year through the West. On September 8, and in Milwaukee, most appropriate, of course, since the Braves were in second place, they clinched the pennant. Craig and Spooner shared the pitching. The Dodgers battered the enemy pitchers that Charlie Grimm threw at them, starting with Bob Buhl. The final score was 10-2. When the game was over, the Dodgers topped the National League field by 17. In Brooklyn, the fans may have saluted the victory with beer and whisky. In Milwaukee, which is proud of its brew, the Dodgers dunked each other in beer and champagne.

As prescribed by the schedule, the Dodgers played out the season. Winning one day, losing another, dropping three and a half games of their lead, yet not caring, winding up with 98 games won, 55 lost and a percentage of .641. All the while with their minds on the World Series, wondering which club they would meet as the Yankees, the Indians and the White Sox grappled, hands clutched tightly around one another's throat, for the American League pennant. From this struggle emerged the Yankees.

The Yankees? The Dodgers and the Yankees had met in five World Series and the Yankees had won all of them.

"The Dodgers," said Tommy Henrich, who used to be a Yankee, "have the best club in baseball. The Yankees are hurting and limping and their pitching is so thin you can see through it. I pick the Yankees."

"The Dodgers," said Billy Cox, who used to be a Dodger, "will choke up. I know. I was with them when they choked as soon as they heard they had to play the Yankees."

"There is something special about the Yankees," a justly esteemed member of the Dodgers said. "I don't know what it is, but playing them does something to you."

Almost everybody seemed to feel the same way, including the bookmakers, who, almost automatically, made the Yankees the favorites.

The Series opened at the Stadium on September 28. Newcombe started for the Dodgers and was knocked out in the sixth inning. Whitey Ford pitched eight innings for the Yankees and Bob Grim pitched the ninth. Snider and Furillo made home runs for the Dodgers but Joe Collins hit two and they won the game for the Yankees, 6-5.

Always to be remembered from that game was the performance given by Jackie Robinson. That afternoon in the Stadium, Jackie turned back the years crowding upon him and, for the space of roughly two hours and a half, was the Robinson of an earlier day. He made only one hit but it was a triple. He had only two assists but they were dazzlers. And in the eighth inning, he stole home.

When Tommy Byrne, starting for the Yankees against Billy Loes in the second game, not only held the Dodgers to five hits and two runs but batted in the two runs that won for his side by a score of 4-2, the Dodgers obviously were in desperate straits. Many fans and baseball writers were proving to themselves that the National League champions were through and were going home to Ebbets Field to die to the raucous cries of "Yez bums yez!"

Before the third game at Ebbets Field the Dodgers seemed strained. They were close-mouthed and when they spoke there was no humor in what they said. These were not the free-and-easy heroes who had cuffed their way through the pennant race. They were two down to the Yankees and they were inclined to be surly. Even the photographers, whom all ballplayers count among their best friends because they give them pictures for nothing, were wary of them. One of the players, speaking to a reporter about another member of his staff, snapped:

"I read what that fat ——— wrote about me! Wait till I see him! I'll tell him to his face what I think about him!"

"Fine!" the reporter said. "I'll tell him you want to see him."

So he did and the reporter who had given offense to the player by what he had written the night before walked up to him and said: "Look, you. I may be fat but I'm not a ———. All I wrote about you was the truth and you know it."

"All right! All right!" the player said. "I'm sorry. I shouldn't have said it! Let me alone!"

"I will," the reporter said, "if you slobs will pull yourselves together and knock the Yankees' brains out."

And so a friendship, so briefly torn, was so quickly mended. Podres turned the Yankees back, the player who had had the row with the reporter helped out with a timely blow and the Dodgers won, 8-3. Much was made, on the sentimental side, of the fact that Friday, September 30 was Johnny's 23rd birthday and that once before, in 1953, he had pitched against the Yankees in a Series game and the Yankees had given him short shrift— and a hiding as well. But Alston wasn't being sentimental. If he knew it was Johnny's birthday, he didn't let on. And he couldn't be expected to remember what had happened to Johnny in 1953 because that year he was in St. Paul and didn't see the World Series. He started him for the sound reason that he was in good shape and ready to pitch.

Remembered from this game, too, was Jackie Robinson. He had seven chances at third base. Some of them were rough but he handled them in a manner that made them look easy. He made two hits and one of them was a double. He drove the Yankee pitchers, beginning with Bob Turley, crazy by his bobbing and weaving on the base lines when they were trying to keep their minds on the hitters.

Jackie probably had at least one of the Yankee outfielders in a jittery state because his base running had earlier made the fielder look like a rank busher. In the first game at Ebbets Field, Robinson, running from first on a hit to left field, had conned Elston Howard into throwing to second. As soon as the ball left Elston's hand,

Jackie darted full speed for third. He made it with ridiculous ease.

In the grandstand, Ty Cobb saw the play and said: "Pardon me for saying this, but that's the way I used to run the bases."

And in the Yankees' clubhouse after the game, Howard said: "He loused me. That's what he did. He loused me."

Not again during the Series would Robinson assume the look of greatness. But that day, as on the opening day, he wore it well.

Now the Dodgers were coming to life. In the fourth game they were full alive. Snider, Campanella and Hodges hit home runs. The Dodgers knocked out Don Larsen. The Yankees routed Erskine. But the Dodgers won, 8-5, and the Series was even.

Alston dared to start Craig in the fifth game. The boy didn't last; Labine had to come in to help him out. But the Dodgers beat Bob Grim, the Yankees' starting pitcher. From the jagged edge of disgrace, they had stormed to the lead, three games to two, as Snider hit two home runs and Amoros hit one. In the Yankees' clubhouse when the game was over, Casey Stengel said: "That young feller looked very good." He was speaking of Craig. "If we could see a little more of him, we might be able to figure him out." There was a moment's pause and then he said: "On the other hand, if he could see a little more of us, he might be able to figure us out."

The Yankees won the sixth game, played at the Stadium. They knocked Spooner out in the first inning. The Dodgers, who were rumored to eat left-handed pitchers alive, could make only one run off Whitey Ford, and Bill Skowron settled their hash for them with a home run with two on base in the first inning.

Now the Series was even again but, from a Brooklyn standpoint, in a very different sort of way. With the seventh game coming up and the Yankees apparently riding high, there were untold thousands in New York who bet their shirts that, faced by this rather unexpected challenge, the Dodgers would succumb in sheer terror.

Those who lost their shirts might have saved them if they could have been in the Dodgers' clubhouse after the fifth game and heard Johnny Podres speaking. Johnny was at once elated and depressed because it seemed to him that the Dodgers needed only one more game to win the Series.

"Naturally," he said, "I'm glad that by beating the Yankees tomorrow, we'll be the champions. I can't root against us, even for a day. But I wish . . . and gee, how I wish! . . . I could have one more crack at them!"

And it came about that Johnny Podres's wish came true and there he was again, looking down the distance from the pitcher's box to the plate at the likes of Hank Bauer, Gil McDougald, Irv Noren, Yogi Berra and Bill Skowron as they rose against him. It came about, too, that he defeated the Yankees again. This time shutting them out . . . and yet, always, he must think of Sandy Amoros and the curious twist of fate that put Sandy in left field.

Podres was opposed by Byrne at the outset of this game and Byrne gave up one run in the fourth inning and another in the sixth. He also gave way to Grim in the sixth as the Dodgers struggled mightily to make their run. In the course of the inning, Zimmer was lifted for Shuba as a pinch-hitter. So, when the Yankees went to bat in the seventh, Alston pulled Gilliam in from left field to second base, posted Amoros in left and in so doing, saved the game.

Martin, first up, walked and pulled up at second when McDougald bunted safely. Stengel, disdaining to sacrifice, wanting to keep the pressure on Podres, ordered Berra to hit and now came the play, which Gilliam couldn't possibly have made. Berra slugged the ball to the left-field corner. It didn't seem Amoros could reach it. Martin and McDougald were off and running and Martin was close to third base and McDougald had rounded second when the little Cuban raced into the corner and caught the ball with his gloved hand. Reese had run out into left center for a relay and when Amoros pegged to him, he whirled and pegged to Hodges—and there was McDougald out in the open, still trying to get back to first base. He easily was doubled, of course, and Reese threw Bauer out to finish the inning.

Podres was tired now but, tired or not, he wasn't going to let the Yankees pry this game out of his grasp. He had to face three sturdy right-handed batters in a row, Bill Skowron, Bob Cerv and Elston Howard, and before each pitch he took a deep breath. Then he fired the ball as hard as he could. Skowron and Cerv went out easily. With Howard up, Podres looked down at Campy's signal for a fast ball and shook his head. He wanted to throw a change-up. A change-up it was and Howard grounded to Reese, who picked up the ball, hesitated a moment and then threw him out. The long haul was over. For the first time the Dodgers had won the championship of the world. Alston, after a year's delay, had done what he was hired to do; he had beaten the Yankees.

They'll Always Boo Mickey Mantle

Mickey Mantle is among the most beloved ballplayers of all time. But it wasn't always so. In the 1950s, he was swift and powerful, young and handsome, but he wasn't a legend— not yet, at least—and he wasn't Joe DiMaggio, whose place in center field Mantle inherited in 1952. So Mantle was booed. The summer of '55 he led the AL in home runs (37), and he was booed. He won a batting Triple Crown in 1956, and MVP awards in '56 and '57, and still he was booed. As he wrote the following article, Milton Gross couldn't know the booing would eventually subside, but not until the remarkable events of 1961, when Roger Maris broke Babe Ruth's record of 60 home runs. With his 61st homer, Maris replaced Mantle as the target of Yankee Stadium wrath, leaving The Mick, often hobbled by injury, to become the people's champion.

BY MILTON GROSS

FEBRUARY 1956

AS THE LINEUPS for the Yankee-Red Sox game at the Yankee Stadium were being announced, there were cheers and the usual catcalls when each player's name boomed over the loudspeaker. However, when the announcer said: "Batting third and playing center field, No. 7, Mickey Mantle," the boos rolled across the huge ball park like thunder on a summer night.

It seemed as though all 61,678 people in the Yankee Stadium had been waiting for this moment to jeer the 24-year-old Yankee center fielder even before the game had begun.

In the right-field bullpen, the Yankee relief pitchers, catchers and a couple of reserve infielders had just sat down on the bench. They watched Mantle trotting out to his center-field position, his eyes glued to the ground as though he heard none of the boos.

"What's it all about?" asked veteran Phil Rizzuto. "Why are they on him all the time like that?"

"If you know the answer, tell me," said substitute catcher Charley Silvera.

"If I could figure out the answer," Rizzuto said, "I'd tell Mickey. He'd like to know."

So, of course, would others, who may have little or no interest in baseball or the Yankees' star, but a considerable interest in crowd psychology.

From the beginnings of baseball, players have been booed sporadically, systematically and unmercifully, but few have been booed so unreasonably. Ted Williams caught it, but he asked for it. Ty Cobb once was ridden constantly by opposing crowds, but he incited the customers. On occasion last season, even Duke Snider of the Dodgers and Willie Mays of the Giants felt the stinging wrath of the home stands. The wolves of Philadelphia seldom let up on certain members of the Phillies, and such as Gene Woodling and Al Rosen claim Cleveland fans are unreasonably rough.

In these cases, however, there was a history of animosity or a sudden gorge of resentment that died quickly. In Mantle's case, it seems more than a mere matter of celebrity, chemistry or perverted partisanship. It is simply a reflection of fan unpredictability.

Mickey, after all, should be the popular hero of the standard baseball success story. From earliest childhood, he was trained by his father to be just what he is now. He leaped full-blown from the zinc-mining town of Commerce, Oklahoma, to the Yankees—and the headlines of the nation's sports pages. He is the walking realization of the childhood dreams of untold numbers of our country's youth. He has never had a truly bad season with the Yankees. He is one of the most feared hitters in the American League. He is also the most booed.

"I've tried to figure it out," said Mantle, "but I don't understand it. I try as hard as I can and do the best I can but sometimes it doesn't seem to be enough. It just seems that the fans want to boo and nothing will stop them.

"I'm not complaining," he said. "Ballplayers have no right to complain about the fans' booing. But it sure makes me feel better when they cheer."

"He doesn't have to make a bad play or anything to get booed," Yankee manager Casey Stengel complained recently. "He can do more things better than anybody else, but they give it to him anyway. It's not right."

If it were only a question of right and wrong, the fans might ask what rights they purchase with their tickets. In a sense, this is what made baseball great, because while he is in the stand, every man is a manager. At home or at his job, he may be derided and browbeaten, but in the company of his neighbors in the bleachers, he sits in divine judgment. He may know little or nothing about the technical side of baseball, but he does know what he likes and dislikes. Mantle apparently is one who can bring out the worst in the customers even if he hasn't yet been able to bring out the best in himself.

To find out what the average fan thinks about center fielder Mantle, I made a tour, one day late last season, of the Yankee Stadium bleachers. I tasted a Cuban sandwich, shared a can of warm beer, and was asked how I'd like a punch in the nose, but I came away with a better idea of why the Yankee fans boo a player they should be cheering.

Early in the game, as Mantle came to bat to face Boston's Willard Nixon, a young man took his face out of a can of beer to let out a loud hoot. I asked him why he booed Mantle.

"I got to have a reason?" said Anthony Gregorio, who lives in upper Manhattan.

"Sure, you got to have a reason," said Peter Fasciglione, who sat beside him. "You don't know why. You sit here all the time and give a razz and you got no reason."

"I got plenty reasons," Gregorio answered. "Every time he comes up, the Yankee fans start clapping. When he comes up, they take out the tape measures. What's there, only homers? Don't he ever go for base hits? He can run, but why don't he steal bases? He can bunt, but he don't like to bunt."

"He's got orders to hit the long ball," said John Stokes, a nearby bleacherite, edging into the argument.

"He's nothing. He's overrated," chimed in Anthony LaGreca.

"What do they want from the guy?" pleaded Stokes. "He's overpublicized, that's all. They expect too much from him."

Mantle popped out. Another bleacherite began to chant derisively: "Pop-up! Pop-up! Big out!"

"What do you have against Mantle?" I asked the chanter, who identified himself as Charles Gorridz, a resident of the Bronx.

MANTLE AND CASEY STENGEL

Before he could answer, a bulky man beside him said: "What's it your business, wise guy? What are you, a house dick or something, going around asking people questions? Let the guy enjoy the game. Or maybe you're looking for trouble?"

I identified myself and told the pugnacious fan all I was looking for were reasons the fans were riding Mantle.

"Why not?" the guy said. "You cheer him and he don't do anything anyway. So we boo him. Maybe he'll get mad and hit one of those pitchers when it counts."

The man pulled a Cuban sandwich from his pocket. "Have a piece," he said. He still didn't look friendly, so I took it. "Here," he said, handing me his can of beer. "Wash it down with this and maybe then you won't be asking so many questions."

In the third inning, I had moved my eavesdropping base to the left-field sector of the bleachers. As Mantle grounded out to first, the man next to me gave a loud, piercing hoot.

"He's overrated, that's what," said my neighbor. "We'll take him down a peg. Who does he think he is? He never waves out here or smiles or anything. What are we, stones, he should never show his appreciation?"

I suggested that Mantle undoubtedly heard the booing and was bothered by it.

"Sure, he hears it," the man said, "and maybe it'll do him good. I know it does me good to give it to him. I just don't like the guy any more. I don't like the way he walks. I saw him on the television the other night and I don't like the way he looks. He just rubs me the wrong way. He got all the breaks and what did he do with them? Nothing."

If the bleacherite considered his remarks more carefully, he would realize that Mickey's record is something. He finished last season with a .306 batting average, the league leadership in home runs (37) and with a tie for the leadership in triples (11). His RBI total was 99. It was the third time in his four uninterrupted seasons with the Yankees that he bettered .300. He played in one more game than he did in 1954, yet he hit ten more homers. Comparisons may be odious, even in baseball, but they are inevitable when ball fans get together and compare their favorites, and it is clear that Mickey's brilliance must dim in comparison with, say, Mays and Snider, who also play center field for the other New York teams.

Mays hit 51 homers, drove in 127 runs and batted .319. Snider hit 42 homers, drove in 136 runs and batted .309. In 1954, Willie batted .345 and Snider .341. These are the figures fans recognize. They are the solid meat and drink of the bleacherites, but the customers feed on more than the cold fare of the statistics. They also are aware that spirit, too, makes a ballplayer. They could forgive Mickey his failure to outdo Mays and Snider in the field and at bat. They find it hard to forgive or overlook what appears to be a serious shortage of all-out effort.

It is not a question of courage. Mantle has more than the normal quotient of that. He has played in pain and ill health. His legs have been his torment and he has strained them far beyond the limit that one could fairly ask. What Mantle apparently lacks is a subtle thing—call it ambition, desire, inner drive or what you will. It is not there for those who want to see it, and somehow the fans have sensed it. His Yankee teammates have recognized the lack in Mickey. The management has felt it. The opposition knows it.

It is the cross Mantle must bear, and the injustice of it all is that Mickey not only is the benefactor of his own great talent, but the victim of it. He was the pawn in the Yankees' passion to produce quickly a successor to Joe DiMaggio. The customers were led to expect more than Mickey has been able to produce consistently, and this is his great sin. There is a considerable gap between the realities of Mickey's accomplishments and the publicity of his years in baseball. The fans resent this spread between fact and fancy.

Thus, after a fashion, the fans are not booing Mantle the man, but Mantle the symbol of hysterical ballyhoo. It may be ghastly to Mickey, but it is a ghostly sort of objection that pervades Yankee Stadium. It is the memory of DiMaggio being warmed over at Mickey's expense. Possibly, Mickey cannot see this, but it is so. The person standing in the center of a storm cannot know its violence and Mantle's entire career with the Yankees has been one of turbulence born of his advance notices, his draft examinations and deferments, his osteomyelitis and subsequent injuries and the burden that has been put on him which he cannot or will not accept. He has been asked to carry a load he cannot handle.

It all started in Phoenix, Arizona, in the spring of 1951, but each day in the five seasons which have passed since then have chipped something away from the aura of unreality that surrounded Mickey at the beginning. He now stands exposed and very real and the fans resent it. This is the injustice.

Mantle never asked to be DiMaggio. He never claimed he was. He was barely old enough to cast his first vote when a public park was named for him in his home town, a former coach christened his son after Mickey and the governor of his state designated him an honorary colonel.

These hometown friends, like the writers who first saw him; manager Casey Stengel, who first touted him; Red Patterson, who publicized him; the Yankees, who owned him, have made Mickey what he is. Mantle is scarcely more than an innocent bystander who was molded one way and then pushed another without recognizing what was being made of him.

In 1953, a writer profiling Mantle in a national magazine said: "Mickey could become the successor to Ruth, Gehrig and DiMaggio. Mickey can be as great as he wants to be. The only question is, does he want it enough?"

It was an unfair question. More justly stated, it would have read: Should Mickey be as great as his fabricators want him to be?

By this time, if the timetable prepared by the Yankee front office after their first view of their phenom had run on schedule, Mickey would have one foot in the Hall of Fame, along with the tape measures used to gauge the distance of some of his home runs, the bat he used to hit them and the balls which landed out of this world. The trouble is that Mickey has never quite matched his advance notices, and the phony, furious hurrahs arranged for him. If the customers really want to be fair in voicing their disappointment that the new DiMaggio is more like Vince than like Joe, they should blame those who measured Mickey for immortality when he is purely and simply earthborne.

Mickey has helped Stengel win four of his six pennants, and there are times when the Yankee manager talks of Mantle as though he were a visitation from Olympus. There are others, however, when Stengel hardly can conceal his irritation at Mickey for not matching the zeal of Billy Martin, the efficiency of Yogi Berra or the application of Hank Bauer.

Casey has needled Mickey considerably in the past, but now he is nettled by the fans, who are harassing Mantle with wolf calls. It doesn't appear in Casey's character to be concerned with a few razzes. In a sense, this may be Casey's surrender of his dream that Mantle will be the imperishable monument the manager would leave behind him when he left. Possibly, it is also the end of Casey's campaign to alter Mickey's style; if it is, it is not because Mantle has mastered the few weaknesses which still plague him periodically.

One of these, of course, is his insistence on switch-hitting. Last season, more than any other, Stengel had the weight of statistical evidence to prove to Mickey the foolishness of not deciding to hit righthanded against all pitching. This had been a bitter bone of contention between the player and the manager. From the beginning, Stengel has been a righthanded advocate. However, he felt he would be limiting Mantle's natural bent if he insisted Mickey forego switch-hitting.

Yet last season. Mantle batted .371 righthanded and .279 lefthanded. From his southpaw stance, he struck out 81 times. He fanned only 17 times righthanded. His lefthanded slugging average was .584. Righthanded, it was .676. This is the kind of language even Mickey can understand, but the suspicion exists that Mickey and his manager no longer are speaking the same language.

The untold story of last October's World Series was Mantle's reticence to play, Stengel's insistence that Mickey try, the manager's petulance at Mickey and Mantle's obvious annoyance.

Mickey, of course, came up to the Series against the Dodgers with a pulled hamstring muscle in his right leg. Until the day the Series opened Stengel kept hoping Mantle's injury would heal sufficiently for him to go into center field. For the first two games of the Series, Stengel withheld Mantle from the lineup. Though the Yankees won the first two, Stengel could not hide his disappointment and chagrin that Mantle begged off each morning when he was asked if he could make it.

On the return of the Series to Ebbets Field, with the Dodgers apparently beaten, the strangest twist in the strange career of Mickey Mantle occurred. For the first time in five seasons since being fitted for the shoes DiMaggio once wore so perfectly, Mantle became an object of sympathy in the stands. What he was in his own dugout is something else again.

In the third game, Stengel inexplicably used Mantle in center field. Part of the reason for the use of the crippled player was clear when Mickey homered in the second inning, but in the first inning, there had been an equally apparent reason why Mantle should not have been used at all. Going for a fly ball by Junior Gilliam, Mantle had to make a one-handed grab after a gimpy chase. Ordinarily, Mantle would have been waiting for the ball. In the second inning, therefore, Stengel shifted Mantle to right field where there is less ground to cover. Mickey played there through the rest of the game and the fourth Series game and it was obvious to all in packed Ebbets Field that Mantle scarcely could move enough to get out of his own way. Thus in the fifth and sixth games, Mickey remained on the bench again. It wasn't until he pinch hit—unsuccessfully—in the seventh game against Johnny Podres that Mickey was seen again by the fans.

At that point when he was at his lowest ebb of efficiency, Mickey probably was loved by the customers more than at any other time. They were sorry for him. He was seen as a poor sucker forced to do something he should not have been made to do by a manager who was mad at him. He was not a young god who would pull lightning from the sky. For once, the customers found a common denominator existing between themselves and Mickey. This may never happen again in Mantle's career because he's the kind of big-leaguer who seems destined never to be close to the fans. His reticence is natural; his fear deep-rooted. He's the kind they will always boo. It is not a pleasant prospect, but it is Mantle's future. There is litle he can do about it. He isn't Babe Ruth, Lou Gehrig or Joe DiMaggio. Mickey can only be himself.

The Bewildering World Of Willie Mays

It speaks volumes about Willie Mays that, in 1955, he batted .319 with 51 home runs and 127 RBI, yet his season is regarded as ordinary. The reason for that lies in 1954, when the "Say Hey Kid" won a batting title, league MVP honors and led the Giants to a four-game sweep over Cleveland in a World Series made unforgettable by a "Say, wow!" over-the-shoulder catch of a 425-foot Vic Wertz blast. Mays' feats of 1954 placed him among baseball's hottest commodities of '55. In just his second full season—Mays was a midseason call up in 1951 and missed most of '52 and all of '53 to the army—he was already regarded among the most complete players in the game. By the time he retired in 1972, he would hit 660 homers with a record 7,000 putouts. But most of that was still to come when Roger Kahn sat down to ponder what lay ahead for this rising star.

By Roger Kahn
June 1956

MOSTLY, THIS IS for people who have seen Willie Mays play baseball. People who haven't can only begin to sense, in some vague, cloudy way, what all the excitement is about. When you've said Willie Mays is an exciting ballplayer, you've said it all. Except you really haven't said a thing.

Joe Louis was a hard puncher. Winston Churchill was a smoothie with a speech. Jascha Heifetz plays a nice violin. Franklin Roosevelt was a hard man to beat. That's what it means to say Willie is exciting. It means everything and nothing.

"Listen," a Giant fan will tell you, "Willie can run and throw and catch better than anyone who ever lived and he's the guy who's gonna break Babe Ruth's record." You nod, figure the fan's been eating opium and hurry on your way to the ballpark. If the uptown traffic is light, you arrive in time to see Willie slam a first-inning homer that carries 450 feet. So you're still in shock when he steals a base in the fourth inning, and you're groggy when he throws a man out at home in the sixth, and when he makes that catch in the ninth, you want to look up the Giant fan and apologize, even if you were born and bred in Brooklyn.

But you don't have to apologize. When Willie Mays is right, he is a Giant fan's implausible dream come to life.

This month (May), it is five full years since Willie first hit the majors. He was just 20 when he arrived, and almost unlettered. Willie has learned rapidly in the intervening time. He has married and grown well-to-do. But explaining and understanding him now is no easier than it was when he arrived, mute, nervous and confused.

The private world of Willie Mays often looks like the most bewildering canvas in baseball. Of course, it depends upon how carefully you care to look.

"Willie," reports one Giant teammate, "is great with the jokes when he's going good. That's when everybody starts figuring he's a great guy. But anybody can joke when he's hitting. I've seen Willie when he doesn't go good. He isn't laughing then. He's crying."

"Willie," says Barney Kremenko, a New York baseball writer who travels with the Giants, "is a genius. What Einstein was in his field, Willie is in baseball. That's all. He's a genius."

"Willie," says Tris Speaker, one of the finest centerfielders of all time, "has a lot of ability, and a lot to learn."

"Willie," says Duke Snider of the Dodgers, "is a helluva centerfielder."

"Willie," says Leo Durocher, "is the greatest outfielder I've ever seen."

Seems fairly clear, doesn't it? Mays has occasional moods which trouble a teammate, has occasional lapses which trouble a perfectionist, but for the most part, in the field, he is above reproach.

"But I can handle him at bat," a Cincinnati pitcher once boasted. "I've been throwing at him and that's done it. I've got him ducking high *outside* pitches." (The pitcher is no longer in the majors.)

"Say," argues Roy Campanella, "you may be gonna stop Willie some times, but you ain't gonna stop him all the time, no matter what you try to do."

"The book on the kid is murder," a scout reports. "Pitch him high and you're pitching to his power. He hits a lot of homers off high pitches. Pitch him low and you're pitching to his average. He gets a piece of the low ones most of the time. He makes most of his singles off low pitches."

Again, there should be no confusion. Willie at the plate is formidable. The occasional rumors that a batting weakness has been discovered have always been greatly exaggerated.

"Willie is wonderful to me," Mrs. Sara May, an aunt who raised Mays, confided before her death in 1954.

"He's always sending me money and things. Only trouble he ever gave me raising him was when he used to run off and play ball and leave the dishes he was supposed to wash and dry. At night, if I told him to be home, he was never late."

"Willie is a really nice boy," says Mrs. Ann Goosby, a matronly widow who was a virtual foster mother to Mays in New York. "When he was living with me, he liked what I cooked and he was cheerful and he stayed around home quite a lot."

"People have asked me," reports Marghuerite Wendelle, who became Mrs. Mays last February, "what I thought about marrying a famous ballplayer. But I didn't feel I was marrying a ballplayer. I know Willie. I was marrying a man."

Now a third image of Mays begins to come clear. He is a young man of matchless kindness and virtue.

Obviously, it is not that simple. Controversy seems to be the handmaiden of success. Assuredly, Willie has been successful. Among the negative results: a New York lawyer says Willie is thoughtless, a magazine editor says he is money-mad, and an outfielder says he is pig-headed. The three have reasons which they sometimes cite at length.

Perhaps Mays' kindness and virtue are not really matchless, but neither is he thoughtless, money-mad or pig-headed. He is, first of all, a pleasant youngster with good instincts. How much more he will become in 15 years is a fine question because his potentialities—off the field as well as on it—are so vast. In five years, he has had so much to learn, so many situations to handle, so many people to meet, that the real wonder of Willie is that he has done so much so well. Of all the great and little characters in the bewildering world of Willie Mays, it is Mays himself who often seems to be the clearest thinker.

A trip into this other world begins most properly at the office of Art Flynn, a New York advertising man who is Mays' agent and business manager.

"Willie," Flynn said, at the start of one trip not long ago, "is out in East Elmhurst in Queens. Give him a call out there."

I spent a spring covering Mays' daily routine for a newspaper once, but names are not Willie's strong suit. So on the phone there was the customary problem. "Who?" Willie asked. "Who? What you wanna see me 'bout?"

"A story."

"What kind of a story?" Willie asked. He was on his guard.

"A story about you."

"Well," Willie said, suddenly genial, "I'd like to see you but I ain't dressed, so I can't pose for no pictures."

"I just want to talk," I said. That knocked the props out from under Willie's case. An hour later, I was tapping on the door of an upstairs bedroom at the East Elmhurst house into which Willie moved soon after his marriage.

The cab driver had gotten lost, running up the meter, during the trip out, and what with Willie's lack of enthusiasm on the phone, an expensively wasted day loomed as I stood there in the hall. But as soon as Willie shouted, "Come in," and I opened the door, the situation brightened. "Hey," he said, "I didn't know that was you on the phone. That your name? How you been?"

I congratulated Willie on his wedding, sat down and looked around the room. It was a memorable sight. Mrs.

Mays was out shopping and Willie, sitting alone in the center of a large bed, seemed almost regal. He was wearing pale ivory pajamas as he rested lightly against a red satin headboard. A half finished glass of orange juice was on the night table. At Willie's feet, a big television set boomed unnoticed.

"Man, I been busy," Willie said. "But it's time for me to be settling down. I'm 24 years old." He was 25 on May 6.

For some reason, I thought of cold cash. "You'll make a fortune," I found myself saying, "if you don't get hurt."

"I won't get hurt," Willie said. "You can bet on that."

"What if they throw at you?"

"They can throw at me," Willie said, "but I ain't gonna be where they're throwin' when the ball comes." Willie giggled. His voice is generally a respectable tenor but it goes up an octave when Willie is excited about something, or when he giggles.

"What about running into fences?"

"I practice," Willie said. "I practice not running into 'em. It ain't easy. I bet you never seen me do it."

He paused, then continued. "First couple of weeks of training, I go out to the outfield and run at the fences fast as I can. Then I stop. That way, I get used to running near the fences, know what I mean, but I get used to stopping just in time."

By reputation, Mays is a natural, which means baseball comes naturally to him. The value of running at fences as a training maneuver may be questionable, but it illustrates another fact: Willie's basic attitude toward the game.

"You got to practice," he said. "First you got to love the game, so's you'll want to practice, but you got to go out and try to do different things like I did and you got to practice doing them."

Mays naturally realizes that natural ability, in itself, is not enough. It may be sufficient for a Mickey Mantle to hit 30 home runs; it is not sufficient for Willie to hit 50. Like all great baseball "naturals," Mays studies the game with more than natural intensity.

"Take grounders," he said. "You got to charge 'em if you're an infielder, so you ought to charge 'em in the outfield, too. But man, that ain't real easy. I mean it ain't catching no pop fly." (Mays is easily the best outfielder of the last decade in charging grounders.) "I practice running in on 'em," he said. "I practice that all the time. 'Course, once in a while, one gets by me, but that's a chance you got to take if you want to charge 'em like you should."

When Mays broke in, he had the face of a small boy. Now, as he sat in bed and talked about his profession, what looked almost like the beginnings of jowls were visible. But more apparent was the face-splitting smile and the uniquely eager expression that he had from the day he joined the Giants. A bell tolled softly and Willie answered a stylish tan telephone that rested on the night table.

"Newsreel pictures?" he said. "What kind of newsreel pictures?"

Willie listened intently. "Well," he said, "I don't know nothing about newsreel pictures in the house. You better arrange it with my agent, Art Flynn."

Again Willie listened hard. "Is there money in it?" he said.

The voice on the other end talked quickly.

"Well," Willie said, "like I say, I don't know nothing about newsreels. You call Art Flynn. Yeah, right, 'bye."

As Willie hung up, he seemed embarrassed. "Hey," he

said, "I know about newsreels. I was just telling *him* I didn't know."

"There's no money in newsreels, Will," I volunteered. "They can take pictures of you on the field any time they want."

"I know," Willie said, "but this is different. If they come to the house and take up a day and maybe want to use the pictures for advertising, it's different. Art Flynn, he tells me if they use my picture for advertising, there should be something in it. I don't know. I just let him handle it for me, things like this."

Once a famous theatrical agent was bellowing about the actors he represented. "They're all too damn proud," he said, "to admit that there is anything in heaven or earth they don't know. So they keep getting themselves involved in dumb deals and I keep having to get them out." Willie may not be much at recitations from *Macbeth*, but he is wise enough to know when to plead ignorance. There is a little native shrewdness in him, yet it is almost totally concealed by his basic naivete. To this day, in some ways, he is innocent beyond belief.

When the conversation drifted to contracts, Willie said he disapproved of ballplayers who worried about salary. "You shouldn't fight about how much you gonna get," he said. "You love the game and practice it and play it good and you don't have to worry. The money, it'll come."

To Willie's left was an open closet door that revealed a vast assortment of suits. "I been lucky," Willie said. "Mr. Stoneham is my friend. I don't know about anybody else. I mean I don't know if they's not my friend. It's just Mr. Stoneham who signs me. We never argue how much I'm gonna get. Whatever he says is right is okay with me, because he's my friend."

When Willie was discharged from the Army in 1954, Leo Durocher reported that he signed without even bothering to look at the figure in the contract.

"I showed him where to sign and he signed," Durocher told an audience at a Phoenix hotel that included, if memory serves, four sportswriters, two actors, one insurance man, and Zsa Zsa Gabor. "What a kid. I yelled what the hell was he doing signing without looking at the figure and Willie says, 'I trust you, Mr. Durocher. You say sign, I sign. You say don't sign, I don't sign.' What a kid."

Because of Durocher's tendency to exaggerate, particularly in the presence of Hungarian blondes, the story seemed worth further checking. But at the time, it withstood all tests, except that Willie called his manager "Leo," or "Skip," not "Mr. Durocher."

"I'll tell you about that," Willie offered as he sat straight up in his bed. "Sure I signed without looking. I was getting out of the Army and when you get out, you always get the same pay you got before you went in. That's one time they ain't gonna cut you. But they ain't gonna give you no raise, neither. I knew the money was gonna be the same. What was the sense of looking?"

There is, of course, a law against reducing the salary of a returning serviceman but Mays' continuing faith in the fairness of baseball club owners is both a compliment to Horace Stoneham and a symptom that causes alarm. His wife, older than he and twice divorced, has been judged by some as a woman whose chief marital aim may be to help Willie spend money. According to this picture, Willie is a child in the hands of a femme fatale. As delicately as possible, I mentioned this impression. Willie's answer was instantaneous and frank.

41

"Look," he said, "I don't know what's gonna be for sure, but I think Marghuerite can help me and I can help her so we can help each other. Sure, they're gonna talk about her and me. Same people was talking and writing columns last summer about how I was gonna marry this girl and that girl. Well, they was wrong then like they is wrong now. Oh, I don't know for sure, but I think I know and I think it's gonna work out." He pointed to his chest. "I'm the only guy knows what's in here," Willie said, gallantly.

When we parted, Mays leaned forward in bed and extended one of his large, strong hands. The pajamas were carefully tailored and a monogram stood out from the ivory. "Anytime you wanna talk, you call me up," Willie said. "Good luck to ya, buddy." At that moment, we were great friends. Future phone calls probably will present the same problems as calls in the past.

Charles Einstein, a writer who collaborated with Willie on the book, *Born To Play Ball*, spent countless hours with Mays during the two weeks he probed for material for the book. The sessions were held in a yellow Lincoln, Mays' car that year, and while Willie drove fast Einstein labored tirelessly to keep his subject talking. This is a soul-searching sort of relationship and one in which two people can become very close very quickly.

Less than a week after the Mays sessions had ended, Einstein found himself stuck at one point in the story. He needed a fact and so, he telephoned Willie.

"Hi, Willie,'" Einstein began, expansively, "this is Charley."

"Who?" Willie said.

"Charley. Charley Einstein."

"Oh," Willie said, so flatly that it was obvious the

name had not registered.

"Willie," Einstein shouted. "Charley Einstein. Two weeks in the car—the book."

"Oh yeah," Willie said. "How ya doin', Charley?"

I thought of this going down the stairs. As I passed the living room, I looked in and there, poised gracefully on a window seat, Mrs. Mays sat, doing her nails. We had not been introduced, but she nodded, with a kind of gracious aloofness. Then I passed out of the bewildering world of Willie Mays into a quiet street in East Elmhurst. It took a long time to find a cab.

Whatever clues exist to Mays' future, as he continues to grow and continues to learn, probably lie in the immediate past. There is a lot to be found in places like Powderly, Ala., where Willie's stepfather and mother live, in a bleak house on a dusty, unpaved street. There is more to be found in Fairfield, Ala., a steel-mill town where Willie's Aunt Sara lived and where Willie grew up. But the first hints of what's ahead for Willie lie in bigger towns, like Minneapolis and New York.

For one thing, it is doubtful if he will become overly impressed with himself. That became apparent on they day in 1951 the Giants pried Willie loose from Minneapolis.

This was in the second month of Willie's second season in organized ball and he had played 35 games for Minneapolis. Willie was doing fine but the Giants were doing very little, or so it seemed. (Actually, they were jockeying for position with the Dodgers, craftily moving 13-1/2 games behind in order to set up their late-season drive.) When the call came, Willie was at a movie house, one of his favorite haunts, and after getting no answer at his hotel, the telephone operator traced Willie to the theater. Mays was already a big man in Minneapolis and there was no question what the call was about. So the theater manager stopped the film and walked on to the stage.

"Call for Willie Mays," he announced, prouder than a midget bellowing cigarette commercials.

Mays, who was with a date, sheepishly left his seat and took the call in the theater office. He had been happy in Minneapolis and, at the moment, playing for the Giants seemed a little beyond him.

"Willie," Leo Durocher was roaring over the long distance lines, "pick up your ticket, hop a plane and I'll see you here tomorrow."

Willie didn't want to go. He thought fast. "You're making a mistake," he said. "You don't want me."

"Course I want you," shouted Durocher, who has been known to compare even Class D ballplayers with Charlie Gehringer when under a full head of enthusiasm. "You're just the man I want, Willie."

"No," Mays pleaded. "You're making a mistake."

"What do you mean?"

"You don't want me," Willie said, " 'cause I'm not good enough."

Now it was Durocher thinking quickly. "Willie," he said. "What are you hitting?"

".477," Mays confessed.

"So," Durocher said, "you pick up your ticket, hop a plane and I'll see you here tomorrow."

Actually, Willie has never been plagued by self-doubts but he has tended somewhat to underestimate his own ability. A good many major-leaguers have a habit of falling back on stock, phony phrases such as, "and then I was lucky enough to hit a 400-foot home run." Willie's appraisals of his own shortcomings are more sincere. At Minneapolis, he did not really believe he was going to be overwhelmed by the majors. But neither did he think he was ready to make them with a splash. "Experience," he says. "There was so many fellows in the league with so much more experience than me, how could I be as good as they?"

Willie was called by the Giants on May 24 and the reporter who covered the story for the New York *Herald Tribune* wrote that Willie was "a preposterous rookie." The man in the *Daily Mirror*, Leonard Lewin, had more to say. "Amazin' Willie Mays," Lewin wrote, "who apparently does nothing short of amazing, wrote another amazing page into his short, amazing career yesterday . . . Today he is a Giant. Not only that, he's the regular centerfielder, shoving Bobby Thomson, the best fielding CF in the NL, to left field for tonight's game in Philly. It's amazin'." Lewin was writing with some skepticism, of course. How could anyone have known at the time that Mays was going to be an outfielder of such defensive talents that nobody in baseball save possibly Duke Snider could even make it close?

As Willie can be both shrewd and naive, so he is often both humble and arrogant. He made that emphatic before long. Mays joined the Giants in Philadelphia, where the left-field stands are 334 feet away at the foul line, but fall off quite sharply, and on his first batting practice swing he reached the upper deck. He did the same thing on his next two swings, but in the three games the Giants played at Philadelphia, Willie didn't manage to make a hit. In his fourth game, he came to bat at the Polo Grounds for the first time and hit a home run over the left-field roof. But that was his only hit in his first 26 times at bat. Willie, who'd been a humble .477 hitter, now was arrogant at .038. "It's only a slump," he said. "I been taking a lot of pitches because I want to see what they throw up here. Now I've found out. They're throwing me the same stuff I was belting in Minneapolis. Not many curves, either. They're giving me the sort of stuff I want." By June 15, Willie had pretty well proven his case. He was batting .314.

Two months later he made a play which established him more than any other single thing he ever did in the majors. The Dodgers were tied with the Giants, it was the eighth inning, runners were at first and third, one man was out and Carl Furillo was the batter when Mays came through. Furillo lashed a long drive into right center field and it was only after a long, frantic sprint that Willie was able to spear the ball. The catch was spectacular in itself but Billy Cox, the Dodger on third, had chosen to play it safe. He held up. When Willie caught the smash, Cox broke promptly for the plate.

Willie had made the catch facing the right-field foul line, about as poor a position from which to throw home as can be imagined for a right-handed outfielder. But Willie pivoted violently to his left and without a pause or a look, whipped his arm around and cut loose. The throw carried to the plate on a fly and Cox, who could run well, was retired on the end of an impossible double play. The Giants won the game, 3-1.

Furillo, himself the possessor of a great throwing arm, underscored the wonder of Willie when he grumbled: "He'll never make a throw like that again." He may never have to. The point is, when he had to, he did. It was, by Willie's own description, "the perfectest throw I ever made."

About that time Leo Durocher took a flying leap onto the Mays bandwagon. "He's good for the team," Durocher began a lecture one day. "He kids the guys and they kid him. He's always saying 'say-hey,' and some of the guys are calling him that. He gets out to the ball park hours before a game and he grabs everyone. 'Say-hey,' he says, 'you wanna have a catch?' That's good for a club, all that eagerness."

"So you really think he's great," prompted a writer.

"I wouldn't trade him for Stan Musial, Ted Williams or even DiMag," Durocher said. "They're great, sure, but Willie's only 19 or 20. Look. I been around the big leagues about 25 years. This kid's the best-looking rookie I've ever seen."

From a somewhat cynical point of view, Durocher's relationship with Mays is not hard to fathom. Durocher saw a good thing and moved in. Such is his way. Nor is Willie's fondness for Leo puzzling. "He never yelled at me," Willie recalls, "and if I did something wrong, he'd come tell me nice and quiet. He was a good manager and he was my friend." Almost from the first, in fact, Durocher made Mays his private project.

Leo has hands as quick as a pickpocket's. As a result, he could battle Willie in pepper games—one man throws, the other hits grounders—and almost hold his own. The two played for soft drinks, often bringing in Monte Irvin as a third man, and Durocher ad-libbed the rules as the game went along. Theoretically, a fielding muff cost a bottle of soda but Durocher, usually with one eye on the crowd, made great shows of racking up soda bottles whether or not Willie had muffed anything.

"That's eight Cokes you owe me," he would yell.

"No," Mays would squeal, "that wasn't no miss."

"Eight Cokes."

"Monte," Willie would plead. "He's cheating." Irvin, a dignified player and a man of great reserve, usually said nothing, offered only a smile.

"C'mon," Durocher would bark and Mays, his face twisted like a sorry clown's mask, would resume the game.

The pepper game was the showpiece. Behind it there grew a personal relationship that was a prominent factor in Willie's development. Mrs. Goosby remarked about it before the 1951 season was over. "Willie takes that man's word for just about everything," she said. "He almost won't make a move unless he's talked to him first."

During Willie's rookie big-league season, as he opened eyes all around the National League, Leo Durocher must have been an eye-opener to him. Here, after all, was a man who had started out almost as humbly as Willie, with no money and precious little education. He had come a long way. His wife was a movie actress and he was a terrific dresser, always wearing flashy clothes, and he drove a nice car. Besides, he liked Willie. He never gave it to Willie the way he gave it to some of the other guys on the club. All you have to do for him is hustle and he looks out for you and tells you things and helps you get so's you can make it big like he did.

One unfortunate aspect of the Durocher success story is its hallmark: ruthlessness. A great manager, an able promoter, Durocher still owes a great deal of what he has achieved to his first rule: Don't clutter your brain with ethics. If Leo Durocher had been the only force brought to bear on 20-year-old Willie Mays in 1951, Mays might today have a great many odd ideas. But happily, Durocher was only one of his close friends.

Another was Monte Irvin.

What Irvin was to Willie is probably best illustrated by an incident that occurred three years later when the Giants were playing an exhibition game in Las Vegas. After the game, the team was scheduled to fly out of town immediately, which would give the players no more than a brief chance to lose money at the gambling tables. But one of the engines on a chartered DC-3 developed bugs and as a result the team was unable to get away until a scheduled airliner, with space available, came through at midnight.

One Las Vegas hotel owner, aware of a lively promotion, invited the Giants en masse for a dinner party and promised them the courtesy of the house up to, but not including, the one-armed bandits. After dinner, Mays headed for the floor show which on that particular night featured an operatic tenor of some talent, who poured out his woes through *Vesti la Giubba*, the most dramatic of all the arias in *Pagliacci*.

In case you haven't been spending your spare time at the Metropolitan Opera House, the pitch of *Vesti la Giubba* is that the show has to go on, even when a clown feels like crying, which, by the way, he does, three-quarters of the way through the song. At any rate, Willie listened, enraptured by the aria, announced that it was "real nice" and, after the tenor was through, moved along to the gambling room. He checked a dime slot machine, where Whitey Lockman and Irvin were striving frantically to keep even, then walked over to the dice table.

"You going to play dice?" a reporter in the Giant party asked him.

"No," Willie said, with that inevitable mixture of wisdom and boyishness. "I'm just learnin' the game."

Willie had not been standing at the table for two minutes before a hotel official walked over to the reporter. "Tell your friend to move away from the dice table," the official said.

"Why?"

"You know why. They can go anywhere they want, but we don't want 'em mixing with white folks at the tables."

The conversation grew steadily uglier until the reporter pulled a press card and the hotel, not eager for the sort of publicity it was courting, sent out fresh officials to counter the demands of the first. The reporter sought out Irvin, who by this time had run out of dimes and was awaiting the start of the second floor show.

"When did this happen?" Irvin asked.

"Right now," the reporter said.

"Where's Willie?"

"Still at the dice table, I guess."

"He'll only get hurt," Irvin said. "I'm going to get him."

Without another word, Irvin turned, sought out Mays and led him toward the nearest exit.

"Plane ain't gonna leave for two hours, roomy," Willie protested. "What we gotta go for?"

"Come on, Willie," Irvin said. "We'll get the bus lights on and you and me can play some cards."

How much the incident would rankle a man of Irvin's intelligence can be guessed, but rather than make Willie, who was then not emotionally mature, the center of a nasty scene, Irvin avoided a scene altogether. When it came to Willie, Irvin was always gentle.

It must have been puzzling for Mays, at 20, to compare his two friends, Durocher and Irvin. Leo was a lot of fun but Monte was quiet and everybody seemed to respect him. Monte was fun to kid with because he always looked so serious, but once in a while he would get real glum and there was no sense horsing around. Anyway, it was a terrific year. It was a good thing he had come up from Minneapolis. The Giants won the pennant with the most exciting drive in history and everybody, Leo mostly, said they couldn't have won it without Willie.

But the next year made up for the good one. Irvin shattered his ankle during spring training and all of a sudden there was an Army call for Willie, despite his dependents back in Alabama. In the Army, Willie matured a good deal.

Others have had rougher Army hitches, but Mays, like any other private, simply did what he was told. Principally, he was told to play baseball for the Fort Eustis Wheels. He batted .420 for the Wheels in 1952, .389 in 1953 and covered so much of the outfield that the other fielders complained about his poaching. But for the most part Willie was a popular soldier. He was not wildly enthusiastic about military life but a rumor that he went AWOL for a week wasn't fair.

He left his company after getting permission from someone further up the chain of command, who neglected to tell the company commander until a few days had passed. By that time there was speculation that Willie had sneaked back to the Polo Grounds.

On his Army discharge, Willie made a quick and remarkable impression. "I hope to bat maybe .300," he told reporters, "but I never been no .300 hitter in the majors before and that big-league pitching is a lot different from what I been seeing."

"There's a report, Willie, that you're going to ask for a $20,000 salary," a newspaperman said.

"That Mr. Stoneham," Willie said, in apparent terror, "would take a gun to me if I ever asked him for $20,000."

"Well, how did the report get started?"

"You know the way writers are," Willie said, echoing an old Durocher saying. "It don't matter what you say. They gonna write what they want to write anyway."

A columnist moved in. "You mean," he said, confidently, "that you'd be just as happy playing baseball for nothing."

Willie was silent for a moment. "Now," he said, finally, "remember you're saying that, not me, if you're going to write it."

Willie had been thinking in the Army, despite numerous military rules against it. When he reached spring training in Phoenix, he was ready for every press conference. He was even ready to offer advice.

"Hey," Ruben Gomez, the Puerto Rican pitcher, called to him one day. "I sign some paper for that man. You know who I mean?"

"Art Flynn," Willie suggested.

"Yeah," Gomez said. "I sign but I not get money."

"You sure you signed?" Willie said.

"Yeah," Gomez said.

"Well, then don't worry," Willie said. "Long as you signed something, you're gonna get money. Sometimes, it takes a little time, but I find that whenever I sign something I get paid." It's almost a tribute to the human race that somebody can be alive for 22 years of the 20th Century and cling to such a doctrine. For Willie Mays, at any rate, the doctrine applied.

After his two years in the Army, Willie was bound for greater stardom than he ever suspected. Everything seemed to mesh at once: the basket catch, seven more pounds of home-run muscle, more consistency against curve balls. Before spring training ended, he was being billed as the star from outer space. Before the season ended, he had locked up the Most Valuable Player award. But he had also run into a sort of personal crisis.

"Willie," Art Flynn once explained it, "suddenly stopped being just another good ballplayer. He became the hottest thing since Babe Ruth. DiMag was extremely popular. Musial and Williams are consistently big. But no one gets the concentrated rush for appearances and everything else Willie got when he got hot in 1954."

Frank Forbes, a New York state boxing judge who is one of the Giants' numerous liaison men to Willie, hinted at another aspect of the problem. "When he first came to New York, he was nothing but a kid," Forbes said, "but he had a likeable, wonderful personality. He was a little bewildered because you don't get much sophistication in a southern state, but by 1954 I don't think anything scared him.

"But I remember one week when reporters started asking him a lot of statistical things like will he break Babe Ruth's record and things like that. He didn't come out and say anything but these questions put things in his head and I noticed that week he was trying for the long ball more often and so he was striking out more than usual."

The transformation to superstar was not painless. The better Mays got, the greater the fuss Durocher made about him: By midseason there were resentments on the club so obvious that even casual observers noticed.

Once after one of Willie's best days, two newspapermen sought exclusive interviews at the same time.

"I'll talk to Willie when you're through," the first one said.

"The hell with that," said the second. "I won't talk to him with you around."

Pretty soon, the journalism seminar turned rough and Willie scooted off to Durocher in honest distress. "I'll talk to 'em, I'll talk to 'em," he said. "What they fighting about me for?"

"Don't worry about the writers," Durocher said, generously. "The hell with them. Get dressed and go home."

The tableau was enacted before most of the Giant squad. Willie wasn't the only man on the team but to some of the players it seemed that impression was spreading. "Look," Willie said, "when I worry I don't play good and when I read the papers too much I worry, so I don't read the papers, 'cept once in a while." This sort of talk struck some of the Giants as a little precious; particularly those Giants who were getting their names into newspapers only in fine print.

There was a coterie of Mays detractors on the club, small but bitter. What prevented them from getting more numerous was Willie's wonderful talent. It is Chuck Dressen's favorite race-relations theory that no white ballplayer ever resents a Negro helping him to a World Series share, even if the white is a volunteer worker for the Klan back home in Dixie.

So what helped Willie withstand the growing pains of '54 with his teammates was ability. What helped him with the press was his odd charm. After the first game of the World Series, when Willie saved the Giants victory by catching a drive Vic Wertz hit from home plate at the Polo Grounds into the shadow of Yankee Stadium, photographers ringed the steps that lead down from the shower room in the Giant clubhouse. When Willie emerged from the showers, the photographers began to shout in their traditional babel, "Heykidlookaheregimmeasmilewillya."

The gibberish was deafening and Willie wanted time to size up the situation. He had a towel draped around his waist and with a big grin he let it slip off to the floor.

A platoon of photographers screamed more babel meaning, "Listen, Willie, put the damn towel back on. How can I take a picture of you when you're naked? Please put the towel back on."

With careful modesty, Willie gathered the towel about him again. Then the first flash bulbs began to pop and he let it fall. Willie laughed his high-pitched laugh, put the towel on once more and kept it there while the photographers snapped away. It had been a pleasant enough joke, even the photographers admitted. Willie just liked to have a little fun.

When the 1954 season was over Mays had batted .345, but when he started slowly last season after a winter of Caribbean baseball, he was put under continuing pressure.

"Some Hall of Famer," a sportswriter jeered, as Mays went through a long hitless stretch early in the season. "Hold up that bus to Cooperstown." This was inevitable. Mays had not boosted himself, but the Giants, desperate to build up their attendance, had promoted him with all guns. Over-promotion may be what ruined Clint Hartung and slowed the careers of Duke Snider and Mickey Mantle. Whenever the well-promoted athlete slips, there is always someone delighted to announce that he had known the fall was coming all the time. The announcement can be disturbing. Besides, there was a special situation with which Willie had to deal: Durocher was putting him on the spot.

One hot March day in Phoenix, the manager, playing a pepper game with Johnny Antonelli and Sal Maglie, decided Antonelli was not bending for grounders with enough spirit. Just then Willie flitted by.

"That's spirit, John," Durocher said. "What Willie shows. Why, if it wasn't for Willie, you wouldn't have won ten games last year." Durocher was referring to a season in which Antonelli had, in fact, won 21. "Johnny walked off the field," Maglie remembers. "He wasn't the same after that. I mean his heart wasn't in it. Sure, pitching is a business, but you like to feel what you been doing is appreciated. The kid is great, don't get me wrong. But so is Dark and a lot of the other guys. Willie didn't win that World Series by himself."

After the Giants shipped Irvin to Minneapolis, Mays roomed alone last year, but by then the initial threat of his learning the wrong things from Durocher appeared to have passed. When Willie was benched during a slump, he said simply, "Leo knows more 'bout me than I do," which was a gracious way of handling a touchy question. And he did hit 51 home runs, so that he hardly staggered through a lost season. Willie now can take care of himself.

"I know Rigney," he said, when someone asked him about the new Giant manager, "and he's a smart man, a lot like Leo in some ways. I mean people think he's careful all the time, but they're gonna get a surprise. Rigney plays the game a lot like Leo."

Occasionally, there is a search made of Willie's earliest days in an effort to analyze the elements that mix in him. No search has been successful yet. It is a simple story of a poor boy with talent.

Willie Howard Mays, Jr., entered the world on May 6, 1931 in Fairfield, Ala., the son of a fair semi-pro ballplayer, Willie, Sr., who earned a living in a steel mill, and Annie Mays. Soon after the birth Willie's father and mother split, and at the age of three Willie went to live with his Aunt Sara. His mother married again to a man named Frank McMorris and it was probably fortunate that Willie moved in with his aunt. Before she died in childbirth, Willie's mother had ten children by her second husband. They all existed in a five-room house. With his aunt Willie got a good deal more personal attention than his mother could possibly have given him and a good deal more in the way of living quarters as well.

Willie has accepted his rather confused family situation splendidly, assuming a fair share of financial responsibility. Says Frank McMorris: "Willie has always helped us and we needed it. Willie is a good boy." His father is reluctant to discuss money, but friends have pointed out how much Willie has assisted Willie, Sr. "I know he's given him plenty of money," one says. "I remember once he gave him $200 and he's always doing things for his father like putting a roof on his house and such as that."

Willie knows about poverty because in his early life it was always there. He remembers playing ball when he was very young, "with older kids" because there was a neighborhood benefactor who provided bats and balls. But when Willie was a high school halfback, he also had to work in a steel mill. He was a star halfback but in 1948, when he was only a sophomore, he managed to win a job on the Birmingham Black Barons. At 16, that summer, Willie batted .311.

The Yankees sent a man to scout Mays two years later

when he was becoming a baseball star and had graduated from high school. The scout reported that Mays was weak on curve balls.

Jackie Robinson knew about Mays. He recommended that the Dodgers sign him. A scout from Mississippi was dispatched. "Won't do," he reported to the Brooklyn office.

The Braves had a man watching Willie and even made an offer to the Black Barons. But there were strings attached: Willie had to make the majors or the purchase price was to be refunded. The deal, understandably, fell through.

So, almost by default, the Giants landed the biggest gate attraction in baseball. They had assigned a man to watch a first-baseman on the Black Barons. Instead, he watched Willie, and for a flat $10,000 the Giants obtained him. They shipped him to Trenton in 1950 and the first scouting report from there was modest.

"He's a major-league prospect," wrote Chick Genovese, the manager. "Possesses strong arms and wrists, runs good, has good baseball instinct. Wants to learn. Should play AAA ball next year."

A year later, when Willie was playing AAA ball at Minneapolis, Hank DeBerry was sent to scout him further. DeBerry's report is probably unmatched in any baseball files, anywhere. It goes like this: "Sensational. Is the outstanding player on the Minneapolis club and probably in all the minor leagues for that matter. He is now on one of the best hitting streaks imaginable. Hits all pitches and hits to all fields. Hits the ball where it is pitched as good as any player seen in many days. Everything he does is sensational. He has made the most spectacular catches. Runs and throws with the best of them. Naturally, he has some faults, some of which are: charges low-hit balls too much, runs a bit with his head down. There have been a few times when his manager needed a rope. When he starts somewhere, he means to get there, hell bent for election. Slides hard, plays hard. He is a sensation and just about as popular with local fans as he can be—a real favorite. The Louisville pitchers knocked him down plenty, but it seemed to have no effect on him at all. This player is the best prospect in America. It was a banner day for the Giants when this boy was signed!"

As a rule, scouting reports are pretty monotonous stuff, filled with such standard phrases as "could make it if he hits curve ball better." Finding DeBerry's report in the Giant file is roughly comparable to finding a sonnet in the files of an advertising agency.

No more reports followed DeBerry's, for soon after it arrived, there came Willie in the flesh at the Polo Grounds to back it up. Ever since, Willie has been supporting the report and even at times making it appear to be an understatement.

With Babe Ruth, the image everyone recalls is a trot, pigeon-toed and mincing, around the bases after each prodigious home run. With Stan Musial, it is the uncoiling of a swing, beautiful to everyone but pitchers. But with Willie, the image is a little more involved.

To begin, there is a faceless batter slamming a long drive to center field. Willie sprints, loses his cap, twists, turns, stumbles, pats his glove impatiently and finally, with a graceful little shrug, he catches the ball at his waist. No one ever caught fly balls quite like Willie Mays and few have caught them anywhere near as well. He has a ferocious swing and, of course, a great arm, but the thing that has set him apart from other fierce swingers and great throwers is his fly-catching. It is unique.

Mays feels much more sure of himself now than he did when he first hit the majors. "I think," he says, "there is still things I got to learn, but nowhere near as much as there was." In his dealings with people, too, he has grown more worldly. "I been learning how to get along and I got a lot of friends," he says almost proudly. "I mean not baseball friends. Fellows I met up 'round Harlem in the 'Y' and all up there who really likes me." But as he is developing talent, Willie is a developing person. It's a long time since anyone has heard him say "say-hey."

"You got to love the game," he still insists. "Otherwise nobody can teach you nothin'. But I wish there was someone around who every time I made a mistake come to me and said, 'Willie, you done this wrong. Do it this other way the next time.' I never had much whatchucall coaching. I mean most of the things I had to learn myself. But I learned them 'cause I know that no matter how good you get there's always somebody can help you get better."

Mays still may antagonize people this season, as he did in others, by shrewdly wondering about money and naively playing practical jokes, even on teammates who are caught in grave batting slumps. He'll kid a few times when he should be serious and be serious a few times when the occasion cries for humor. But then Willie is only 25 years old.

Like anyone else, Willie falters once in a while, only it usually costs him more than it does the other fellow. One day last summer, Duke Snider hit a shot that squirted through Willie's hands and bounced toward the distant center-field fence in the Polo Grounds. Willie realized

Snider would be home before he could even reach the ball, so he let it roll. But somebody has to chase a loose ball, and rightfielder Don Mueller made the long trot while Willie watched, his hands on his hips. Any player is scolded for standing around, but the storm that fell about Mays was fearful. When a hero gives up, the drums always roll.

No matter how far he goes, it's doubtful if Willie will ever quite accept what is happening to him as entirely true. The dreams he had as a boy in Alabama could not begin to approximate the life that he has actually found with the Giants.

Back when Willie received his Army discharge and flew across the country to join the Giants at Phoenix, Leo Durocher hugged him repeatedly for joy and for the news photographers. When the hugging was over, Monte Irvin walked over and gave Willie his hand.

"He's shaking hands with the pennant," a Giant fan proclaimed in the wild enthusiasm of the moment.

"Hi, roomy," Irvin said, quietly.

"Hey, Monte," Willie said.

Irvin smiled at Mays, then said, "Roomy, how's your game?"

Willie shook his head. "What you mean my game, Monte? You talking about pool?"

"No, Willie," Irvin said. "I'm talking about your game, about baseball."

"Oh yeah," Willie said, a little surprised. "My game baseball. I'm ready any time."

Of such is made the bewildering world of Willie Mays.

Has Eddie Mathews
Grown Up?

Eddie Mathews was a ballplayer who swung for the fences and shot from the hip. In 1955 he ranked among the game's best sluggers and baddest boys. But if he was baseball's problem child, the Braves were happy to call him theirs, because Mathews was on his way to becoming the greatest power-hitting third baseman the game had seen. He hit 25 home runs as a rookie in 1952 and then had three 40-plus seasons, including 1955, when he hit 41 with a league-high 109 RBI. But by then the 23-year-old slugger had also become known as a hot-head and a night owl who had brushed with the law, sparred with the press, and come to blows with a passenger on a train. So there was good reason for Furman Bisher to wonder if success would ruin Eddie Mathews. It didn't, of course. He ended up with 512 home runs and a place in the Hall of Fame.

By Furman Bisher
June 1955

ONE DAY LAST SUMMER many people in Milwaukee's extensive colony of baseball worshippers reached for the daily paper and the aspirin bottle at the same time. There on the front page, beside the news about affairs in Indo-China, was an item that had blasted its way out of the sports section. It said that Eddie Mathews, boy third-baseman of the Milwaukee Braves, had been arrested in the early morn hours for speeding, running a traffic light that burned a brilliant red and in general giving a traffic cop a bad time. There was also a whiff of high spirits about the story, though when the charge was actually presented it consisted only of a violation of a speed law.

Mathews was eventually fined $50. Manager Charlie Grimm of the Braves charged him $100 more. But $150 didn't cover the whole impact of the small event and the effect it had on the baseball career of this boy idol and the people who idolized him.

"Well," some thought, "there goes another kid shot to hell. A little prosperity, a few headlines, then a little booze, some night life and they don't know what to do with themselves but run wild."

Some writers implied that home-run hitting and carousing seemed to be roommates, pointing up similarities between the cases of the boy Mathews and Babe Ruth, who never seemed to grow up. The New York Yankees had been testing their patience with the antics of another prodigy, Mickey Mantle, who appeared to slug as well on the night-life circuit as at the ball park. There was almost a unanimous whistle-blowing on the younger generation of athletic celebrities. In Milwaukee itself, where the Braves had seemed incapable of anything less than heroism, sports editor R. G. Lynch leaped on Mathews' strong frame with sharpened spurs and gave the home-run slugger a severe going-over in his column, "Maybe I'm Wrong."

In this case, it seemed that the column title was more accurate than usual, for this is what had happened:

After a Sunday doubleheader, Mathews had gone out to dinner at the home of pitcher Bob Buhl and his wife.

There was some beer before a late dinner, a couple more after dinner, and, at 2 a.m., Mathews started back to his apartment. He heard the whine of a patrolman's siren, to which he responded much as a boy playing hookey from school. He scurried for shelter. He doused the headlights, sassed the officer that arrested him and later threatened a photographer in court. In almost every respect, Mathews reacted like a recalcitrant child being led home by the ear. It wouldn't have been so bad, except that he was arrested by probably the only police officer in Milwaukee who had never seen the Braves play and didn't know Eddie Mathews from Christy Mathewson.

At the time Mathews didn't realize the extent of his public error. Now he does. He can even laugh about it, though with relief, not in jest. "It was all my fault because of my bullheadedness," he said one day this spring. "Driving with my lights off, sassing the cop, and then threatening that photographer. Know what I told him? 'You shoot that picture, and I'll break your arm off.' It was like a game. He'd get ready to shoot and I'd turn around. Honest, it was more like a gag, and I was laughing most of the time. I just never realized they'd make so much out of a little thing like that."

This was Mathews' first jolting introduction to his new rating as a celebrity. The moment he hit his 40th home run in 1953, he surrendered his right to privacy. This he has had extreme difficulty in accepting, but now the realization is taking hold. Now he views that encounter with the law as he might the first trip to the woodshed with his father. It was one of the most important steps in the process of his growing up.

"It's probably one of the best things that ever happened to me," Mathews said. "I'm sorry it had to happen, but I guess that's the best way for me to look at it."

Two other important steps in the maturing of a National League baseball star who is years ahead of schedule in the record book included the death of his father and his own marriage, all events of the critical year of 1954. In one there was sobering sorrow, and in the other a new kind of happiness—happiness that came wrapped in responsibility.

Last August while the Braves were in Pittsburgh, Mathews got a wire from his mother in Santa Barbara, California. His father had died. "My dad and I always were close," he said. "He'd been in the hospital with tuberculosis off and on since 1951, but still it's a shock when you first realize he isn't here any longer. My biggest regret is that he never got to see me play in the big leagues."

On September 27, the day after the close of the major-league season, Mathews was married to a young lady named Virjean Lauby of Marshfield, Wisconsin. This coming July or August, he will become a father. All of these things are contributing to the maturing of a boy who has always had tremendous baseball talent and long has been acclaimed for it but who only now is learning how to carry his fame gracefully.

"What everybody seems to forget," says John Quinn, the genial and understanding man who is the general manager of the Braves, "is that when they're dealing with Mathews, they're dealing with a boy. Here he is 23 years old and he's already been in the major leagues three seasons. He has already hit 112 home runs. Do you know that only one other player before him ever hit that many home runs at such an early age? Mel Ott did it with the Giants, but it took him five years to accomplish what Mathews did in three. Some of these newspapermen who've found him hard to get close to forget that they're dealing with a boy who's young enough to be their own son."

There have been insinuations that Mathews took lessons in press relations from Ted Williams. He is a hero-worshipper himself, you see, and Williams always has been his idol. They have never met (or, at least, had not when I talked to Ed a few weeks ago). When they do, Mathews will be a shy boy, ill of ease in the company of such a renowned athlete. Until recently, Mathews had known little about Williams' running war with the press. You don't get a lot of this kind of news out of sport sections, unless you're an expert at detecting undertones. Besides, Mathews isn't a great sports-page reader. He goes for books with a Western flavor. ("I like a lot of shooting.")

Mathews was, for instance, puzzled by the critical nature of Lynch's post-arrest column. A New York columnist added to his mystification. He virtually called Mathews a menace to boyhood. "You'd have thought," he said, "that I had stuck up a bank."

As feverishly as little Don Davidson, the Braves' publicity director, has worked to smooth out relations between Mathews and the press, he hasn't been able to keep up with the multiplying demands on the young man. "What am I supposed to do?" asked the young slugger. "They come up to me when I'm in the batting cage and ask me questions. You remember when Joe Adcock was beaned last year? Some guy comes up while I'm taking batting practice and asks me what I think about it. I guess I've been asked the question about breaking Babe Ruth's 60-home-run record ten thousand times. What am I supposed to say? Sure, I'd like to break Ruth's record. I'd like to hit 60 homers every season. But that's not my goal. I don't go up there to hit a home run every time. I want to get base hits that win ball games, and if it turns out that I hit 60 homers, good. But that's not my goal."

(Charlie Grimm has the answer to the stock question about the 60 homers. "There's only one guy that ever hit 60," he says, firmly. "There's only one guy in the major leagues now who can break it—Mathews. He's the only guy around that's that kind of hitter.")

Mathews is no pop off. He can understand why a sportswriter would ask Del Crandall, the articulate captain and catcher of the Braves, what he thinks about the March 1 spring training deadline, or does he consider umpires necessary. Mathews doesn't understand why they ask Mathews.

"What can a guy like me tell them that would be worth printing?" That *was* his attitude. Now, a responsible citizen and householder approaching fatherhood, he sees his new responsibility. "I'll try to answer their questions, but they've got to realize that baseball comes first with me. I'm not the most pleasant guy to be around after I've gone oh-for-four."

There's a trace of hot temper in Eddie. His brown eyes spit a little fire now and then, such as the time he climbed the dugout steps in Milwaukee and made jeering gestures after the official scorer had failed to give a teammate a hit. Or such as on his wedding day, when another photographic unpleasantness arose, upon which Mathews hissed: "If I wasn't getting married, I'd eat you out right here." These are tantrums of a boy who is gradually growing into a man.

Actually, it might be nearer the truth to say that Mathews is afraid of newspapermen. Their questions often seem to tie his tongue—and then his temper takes charge. Some people say it's because he's an only child, accustomed to pampering and parental petting. Others say it's because he's no mental giant, which he isn't. At the same time, however, this Mathews is by no means a big, dumb kid. His formal education ceased after high school, but he's learning his lessons in how to live every day he reports to the ball park. He could have gone to college, several of them as a guest of the management. Football scouts hammered on the Mathews' door with scholarships in their hands, because young Eddie was a standout halfback at Santa Barbara.

"I didn't want to go to college, though," he said. "I never did like to study. I don't like to read except what I want to read. I never had any idea of doing anything but playing baseball."

This is where his wife makes a valuable contribution to his advancement. Virjean spent two years at Wisconsin State College in Eau Claire. She is a bright, personable young lady of 20, who handles herself and her celebrity husband with considerable social finesse.

Charlie Grimm seemed genuinely surprised at the suggestion that Mathews might not be enjoying the best of relations with the press. He was surprised, too, that one of the pocket-size magazines had branded Mathews one of baseball's problem children.

"That's funny," he said, meaning odd funny, not amusingly funny. "He's never been hard to handle. He's been as regular as can be. He's done his work, taken his bumps and never complained. That was unfortunate, that thing last summer. I had to do something, so I fined him, but that was the end of it. Last year when I experimented with him in the outfield, he took it without a whimper. He'd try any position I told him to."

That was one occasion on which Mathews did use the press to his advantage. He deliberately planted the quote that he'd like to have a fling at the outfield. This was before the Braves made the trade for Bobby Thomson. "I did it," he said later, "to take Charlie off the spot. He had been gigged a lot about the idea, and I just wanted them to know it was okay with me."

There's a lot of timidness in Mathews, except when his bat is in his hands. And he also has a lot of that stuff Arthur Godfrey made famous—humility. Joe Taylor, the Braves' equipment manager, recalls that on Mathews' first visit to the spring training quarters at Bradenton, Florida, in 1950, he was one of the boys in the back room. "There were two rooms in an old shack back of the regular clubhouse," Taylor said. "We put some of the greenpeas back there, Mathews among them. He never said a word about it. I just took a liking to him, a kid straight out of class D, because of the way he took things. We made a trade during spring training and some locker space was left open in the big clubhouse. You never saw such a look of appreciation on a kid's face as when I told him that he was moving in with the varsity."

Taylor is probably Mathews' closest friend, a sort of a Ted Williams-Johnny Orlando situation. Taylor was the best man at Mathews' wedding. Mathews takes generous care of his friend with handsome tips and other considerations.

"That's another thing," Mathews said. "They took this vote of the baseball writers a couple of seasons ago, and I was voted the worst dresser and the poorest tipper on the team. That really burned me up. I don't run around handing out $10 tips, but I try to be as generous as possible and still save some money. No, I don't funnel the dough out to make a big show, and I don't have a Cadillac drive up to the hotel door to pick me up. I see a lot of ballplayers do that, but I don't think it makes sense. I'm not much for showing off."

What he didn't say was that he has contributed heavily to the support of his family, people of average means. From 1950 until his death his father, Edwin Lee Mathews Sr., battled tuberculosis. He was unable to contribute to the family income. Mrs. Mathews, a lady so young-looking and attractive she appears to be Eddie's older sister, works in a delicatessen. But the bulk of the income has been returned by the fat end of the big bat that Eddie Mathews has been swinging since he joined the Braves' High Point-Thomasville farm club in the Class D North Carolina State League in 1949.

First, though, there had been a brief inspection visit in Chicago with the Braves, then operating out of Boston. Johnny Moore, an old National League outfielder, had signed Mathews to a small bonus contract the night he was graduated from high school. It was a green, wide-eyed 17-year-old who caught the train for Chicago and who walked with the caution of a cat on a tin roof into the batting cage at Wrigley Field for his first major-league swing that June.

"Do I remember him?" Del Crandall chuckled. "How can I forget him? I hadn't been in from Evansville so long myself, but already I was a big-leaguer! I remember this big kid taking seven or eight swings. He never got the ball out of the cage. We were all looking at one another and yakking. 'Who's that punk? Some guy they gave a $50,000 bonus!'"

Johnny Cooney, the coach, remembers Mathews'

introduction with more tenderness. "He took five swings and had five misses, but he had that nice, smooth stroke. You knew there was something there."

If there were many doubts about it, they were cleared up by Eddie during his first season in the National League. In 1952, he hit 25 homers with the Braves and what few people in Boston talked about the club that year talked mostly about the Braves' kid third-baseman.

The transfer to Milwaukee that set the woods of Wisconsin afire in 1953 wasn't in favor of Mathews the home-run slugger. County Stadium wasn't built for left-handed home-run sluggers. Eddie struck 47 homers his first season in Milwaukee, but publicity director Davidson has a set of figures that make an impressive statistical attack on Ruth's high-water figure. "If he had hit the same drives in Boston that he did in Milwaukee," said the tiny publicist, "he would have hit 18 more home runs and he would have broken Ruth's record."

Once you get past their mutual left-handedness and their knack for the home run, there isn't much of a parallel between Babe Ruth and Eddie Mathews. There is only a slight trace of the boisterous rowdy that was Ruth in the make-up of Mathews. Ruth had an enormous appetite for living, a highly developed disregard for rules and regulations and little or no devotion to responsibility.

"He lived 100 years in 50," said Duffy Lewis, the traveling secretary of the Braves and apparently the only living man who saw Ruth hit his first and last home runs in the major leagues. He and Babe were teammates both with the Red Sox and Yankees. Later, he worked in the Red Sox front office, and so he has seen Ruth, Williams, and Mathews close up, and thus qualifies as an authority on all three sluggers. "Babe never changed," he said. "He was still the same kid when he left as when he came to the big leagues. He was just a big, happy-go-lucky guy. He had little mannerisms that made him popular with the fans, that pigeon-toed walk, that big belly, the bowing and tipping his cap, and always that big smile of his.

"Williams lives inside himself. He has no feeling for the public. I don't think I ever saw him tip his cap when he crossed the plate after hitting a home run.

"Mathews is a different personality altogether. He's a new model. He's serious about baseball. He's got a great sense of responsibility to baseball and his family. He takes care of himself. He doesn't get as close to the fans as Babe did, but I think he will when he's older. I think he'll come along and be almost as popular as the Babe. After all, you know, there was only one Babe."

Mathews, according to Lewis, fits in somewhere between Ruth and Williams on the personality range. He's still a raw, unpolished gem whose real luster as a personality hasn't been scratched yet. Neither, it seems, has his tremendous potential as a magnetic baseball attraction.

Frank Scott resigned as traveling secretary of the Yankees a few years ago to become a ballplayers' agent. He now has 88 men in his stable, and though Mathews has been a client for only two years, he already ranks among the top six in demand for testimonials, endorsements and public appearances. The other five are Stan Musial, Yogi Berra, Duke Snider, Robin Roberts and Mickey Mantle—all save Mantle many years Eddie's senior in the major leagues.

Mathews should be in the $50,000 income-bracket this year. He signed a two-year contract with the Braves after an hour's conference with Quinn in Florida. His salary is estimated at $35,000. He will make in the neighborhood of $15,000 for saying he smokes a certain brand of cigarettes, saying he wears a certain kind of shoes, saying he eats a certain kind of breakfast food, and in other forms of name-lending for a fee.

"He's got a potential," says Scott, "of making more money on the side than any ballplayer in the last ten or 15 years. Last year, he made around $10,000, but he could have made twice that much. When a guy's got the potential of breaking the home-run record, you don't want to get him tied up until he can command the big price.

"I can tell you this, he's one of the easiest, nicest guys to work with I've ever had. I'd say he's in the Musial class, and that's a class by itself. The New York writers, though, they just don't understand him at all.

"Let me tell you a little story. On the Braves' second trip into New York last summer, I went over to Brooklyn to see Eddie. At the time, his father was back in the hospital and on the verge of death. The kid was awful upset, his father about to die and his mother having to bear it alone. These two photographers walk up and ask to take his picture. 'I just don't feel like it now, fellows,' Eddie said to them. 'How about later?' Well, you know how that would go over with a couple of photographers. Fortunately, I happen to be standing there and I explained to them. But think of the times he felt like that, and there wasn't somebody there to explain for him."

It was a tremendously taxing summer for Mathews. He had cruised through the traditionally hexing sophomore season with acrobatic ease. But the anvil fell on him his junior year. He had a serious misery in the back in spring training. Then came the infamous night ride and the race he lost with the traffic cop. Later, his father died, and after returning from the funeral, he split a finger in Chicago. All told, he missed 23 games and lost his home-run title to Ted Kluszewski. But Eddie still managed to blast 40 out of the park, drive in 103 runs, bat .290 and arrive at a new effectiveness in the field.

For all his setbacks, there was one rewarding experience that made the summer worth living. One day, as he left his apartment for the ball park, he found his automobile wedged in by the impromptu parking effort of two young ladies. They sat in the front seat of their car, poring over a map, trying to locate the street address of a friend.

"Can I give you a hand?" Mathews asked. It turned out to be the most fateful question he ever asked. One of the girls was Virjean Lauby, daughter of a Marshfield appliance dealer, making her first visit to Milwaukee in ten years and driving for the first time in a city of such size.

Eddie helped the girls locate the address. He also invited them to come see the Braves play. They accepted. They had dinner together after the game with some of Mathews' relatives from Dallas, Texas, and the romance was building. Virjean went home to Marshfield to tell her family about the nice young man she had met. Her two younger brothers immediately began to display new respect for their sister when they discovered that she'd been dating Eddie Mathews of the Milwaukee Braves.

"I'll have to confess that I didn't know who Eddie was," said the bright-eyed Virjean, her deep brown hair clipped short in one of these Italian hairdos. "I knew he was a baseball player or something. I remembered that I'd heard the name like I might hear the name of one of those foreign diplomats that's always on the front page. I guess I was one of the few people in Wisconsin that hadn't seen the Braves play before."

She has since realized that she tied herself to a comet when she married her celebrated husband, but she has yet to comprehend the immensity of the plot.

"I'm married to a baseball player," she said, half shrugging. "What's so unusual about that? Other wives are married to baseball husbands. We've bought a house. We've got a dog. We're going to have a baby. We plan to live like normal human beings."

This plan fits in with Mathews' only desire for living. It was a year ago last spring that he explained one day what he had in mind for the future. "I want to get married," he said. "I think it's the thing to do, and I look forward to having a wife. I'm not shopping around, but if the right girl comes along, I'm ready to get married. It looks like a good life to me."

Last winter, the young Mathews made another move toward becoming solid, taxpaying citizens. They bought a red-brick ranch-style home in the Brookfield suburb of Milwaukee. Next came the purchase of a German shepherd named Toby. After the return to Milwaukee, Mathews headed for the hardware store and equipped his garage with a set of garden tools. He's now one of the leading yard putterers on his street.

The fishing bug bit Eddie early last year, an occasion marked by near disaster in Texas. Strictly a land-going sailor, Mathews upset a boatload of friends near Dallas and almost drowned the lot. Last winter, he learned about the joys and the rigors of hunting. Out in Santa Barbara, there is an investment counselor who is directing a portion of his savings into stocks and bonds. In other words, every important move he has made since the night the Milwaukee traffic cop ran him in has been aimed in the direction of maturity and sound living.

It is true that once upon a time this trend seemed absolutely foreign to Mathews, a fun-lover then experimenting with the joys of life. Eddie is a handsome young man with soft eyes, and wherever he went he found himself high in feminine demand. He learned that he could call his own signals, and on his minor-league stops, this was pleasant. When he reached the majors, however, he became a cornered prey.

While the Braves were still in Boston, a young woman came to the club office and charged that Mathews was the father of a baby she was expecting. She threatened a suit, but her enthusiasm for the charge faded rapidly when it was proved to the satisfaction of the Braves' management that Mathews had never seen the girl before.

It is quite reasonable to assume that with the switch to Milwaukee, where baseball became the driving force of the community, the intensity of feminine demands on Mathews' time grew in proportion. Eddie and Joe Adcock shared quarters at a downtown hotel the first year, but eventually they lost all traces of privacy. Last year, Mathews took an apartment by himself, equipped with an unlisted telephone number. Circumstances such as these, his envy of the happy married life of the Bob Buhls, the Chet Nichols' and the Joe Taylors, and his chance meeting with Virjean increased his enthusiasm for marriage.

It isn't possible to complete such a story of so complex a young man without going behind the clubhouse door. In there, you're liable to find Mathews playing the ukulele, or pitching little Don Davidson under the shower with his clothes on, or singing out loud in song in a voice strong but untrained, or listening to one of the Braves spin a yarn—but seldom ever the spokesman himself.

"He isn't a bull artist," said Jack Dittmer, the second-baseman. "On the road, he's pretty quiet. You'll see him get his western book and go to reading. He and Buhl are always going to those shoot-'em-up movies. They go for either wild westerns or old gangster shows."

On the other hand, if it has been a bad day, you'll find the moody Mathews sitting in complete dejection. His shoulders will be rounded into a slump, the wet under-flannels clinging to his sweaty body. He'll be sucking on a soda or a beer. He won't be good company. He wounds easily on such occasions.

"They say don't take the game home with you," he said. "How are you gonna keep from taking it home with you, if it's your life and you've had a bad day?"

Charlie Grimm calls him "just a helluva guy with his teammates. He's what I call a team value ballplayer. His old cap still fits him."

During the winter after his rookie season, Mathews returned to Boston to be the guest of honor at a banquet. The manager of a restaurant in Boston introduced him to his Irish niece, a particularly ardent Red Sox fan.

"Oh," she said, "you play for that seventh-place team down the street." She continued the rib for several minutes, upon which Mathews, doing a slow burn, turned on her and snarled:

"Look, sister, the Braves are my ball club. Even if they finish tenth, they're still my ball club. You've got no right to talk about them that way."

The deepest cut of all was delivered to Mathews by a former short-time member of the Braves who now lives in Santa Barbara. Early in young Eddie's Boston career, this player called the elder Mathews with this ominous warning: "You'd better do something about your son before he becomes an alcoholic. I got friends that say he's trying to drink all the booze in Boston."

It was a crazy, vicious rumor, for this isn't the kind of Mathews they knew in Boston, or know in Milwaukee. It also wasn't the kind of son that Ed Mathews Sr., had reared out in Santa Barbara, as he found out to his own satisfaction.

One day in Florida last spring, Eddie tried to explain himself. It was one of those tropical, rainy days given to serious thinking, and he sat before the locker that said "41 Mathews" and spoke with a good deal of feeling. "I try to be sensible," he said. "I try to be conservative in the things I do. I try to keep my feet on the ground, and that's not too hard, because I say to myself that I'm doing what I always was doing—just walking up to the plate with a bat in my hand and swinging.

"I'll admit, though, this all seems like a dream to me, big salary, major leagues, and people coming up to ask me if I think I'll break Babe Ruth's record. Sometimes I wake up in the morning and wonder if this really is happening to me. But I don't think about it too much.

"I try to be careful of my conduct. I've found out by this time that the smallest thing I do wrong can grow into the wildest story. I've been careful and I've tried to behave myself, honest. I know what's right and what's wrong. I'm just going on trying to do what I've done before."

There's all manners of greatness in him. It's just a question of when the man completely takes over from the boy.

The High School Kid Who Could Play Pro Now

It is common today for high school kids to jump directly to the NBA. But there was a time when it was ridiculous to suggest that a teenager—no matter how big and talented— could compete with pros. Wilt Chamberlain, 18, was the first to challenge that perception when, in 1955, he came loping out of Philadelphia's Overbrook High School with a game that left pro scouts drooling. As recounted by Irv Goodman, Chamberlain's dazzling high-school years ignited a frenzy among college recruiters and NBA managers. He opted to take his immense talents to the University of Kansas, while, in an unprecedented move, the NBA allowed the Philadelphia Warriors to select Chamberlain in the 1955 territorial draft (which had previously been restricted to college players). After starring at Kansas, Chamberlain spent a season with the Harlem Globetrotters before joining the Warriors in 1959 to begin his record-shattering NBA career.

By Irv Goodman
March 1955

WILT CHAMBERLAIN IS a skyscraping, 18-year-old schoolboy with a thin mustache and a swelling price tag on his head who just might be the best basketball player there is. "Just might be" is the cautious phrasing of a reporter seeking an editorial hedge. Others are less timid. One coach, of some repute and conservative mood, says Wilt is as good as George Mikan was last year or the year before that. Another coach, of equal repute but more courage, says he's better.

In the recorded history of the game Dr. Naismith designed in a YMCA gym in Springfield, Massachusetts, it is doubtful if there ever has been such praise for a young, untested basketball player as there is for the towering senior of Overbrook High School in Philadelphia. Nobody can watch Wilt play and come away without being astonished—or at least somewhat impressed.

But then you probably have never seen Wilt Chamberlain play basketball. He is something special in a game devoted to unusual athletes. He can run and shoot and pass and dribble and jump. He is strong and smart and tough and determined. His legs are thin and powerful, his hands are large and firm. He loves to play and he wants to win. He weighs about 230 pounds. He stands about seven feet tall.

But don't let the height fool you—don't fall into the common trap of labeling him a mere basketball goon who parlayed proximity to the basket into success. Wilt is unusual—if a seven-footer can be unusual on other counts. He was good before he was tall.

The history of the big man in basketball has been one of height first, ability—or striving for it—second. The way it usually seems to work is a coach, in high school or college, spots a kid bending over to walk through a doorway and quickly hands him a basketball and sends him out on the court to learn the game. Wilt, however, was a good little man—or, at least, moderately-sized man—before he became a good big man.

None of this should suggest that his height hasn't helped him. It has. It has made him one of the most sought-after high-school basketball players in the shadowy annals of sports recruitment. Only, and this is the point we want to make, Wilt does so many things well that he would have been a good ballplayer if he had been a mere six-footer. He runs like a little man (he has done 880 yards in under two minutes), he has basic court savvy, he can hit with a one-hander from the corner, thrown off the ear, or with a two-handed set from the outside. He passes well out of the pivot, learns and develops quickly, and thinks in sound basketball terms. It is when all of this is packed in a seven-foot frame of bone and muscle that the total talent becomes awesome and most desirable.

Everybody is after Wilt. The pros want him to join them right after high-school graduation without bothering about the four-year stopover at some college. "He can finish his schooling on the money he'll make," someone close to the National Basketball Association suggested. (At least one pro team would be willing to pay him $12,000 as a first-year man, its owner says.) Abe Saperstein wants him to go on the road with the Harlem Globetrotters. Wilt, a bit of a ham on and off the court, has displayed some typical Trotter talents. He can spin and fake, look one way and pass another, thrust the ball with one hand into the face of an opponent and then take it back, shoot without looking, etc. Then, naturally, the colleges want him, too.

At the beginning of this season, Wilt admitted that he had over 100 college offers. Some of the people who have been close to him at Overbrook claim that he had over 100 offers last year when he was only a junior. This year's bids, they say, are mainly renewals, updated with more attractions. What is probably the most unprecedented aspect of the recruitment campaign is that it started two years ago, when Wilt was 16 and a sophomore. It has been building in momentum and attractiveness ever since.

The local Philadelphia colleges were probably the first to approach him. LaSalle, it is reported, has been interested in him since 1953. Basketball people in Philadelphia think that the Explorers stand a good chance of landing him. One point in their favor is that ex-LaSalle star Jackie Moore, who is Wilt's local hero, also played at Overbrook. The argument LaSalle alumni have been giving Chamberlain is that he would be entering a ready-made national spotlight. He would be replacing the supposedly irreplaceable Tom Gola and would lead a standout team that has good prospects for the immediate future at least, in an annual battle for national honors.

Several Midwest schools have been in on the Chamberlain race almost from the beginning. A University of Indiana basketball enthusiast admits he offered Wilt $100 a week, plus the usual scholarship benefits, to join the Hoosiers. The $100 would be payment for an off-campus job, the toughest part of which would be picking up his weekly check. Since then, it was learned, matching offers have been submitted by other schools.

Alumni have been busy taking Wilt on flying trips to their respective campuses. Almost every weekend since the end of last summer, Wilt has been picked up at home on Friday night, flown to the college campus, shown around and deposited back in Philadelphia Sunday night. When we spoke to Wilt about these trips, he was reasonably close-mouthed, admitting only that he had been on the weekend jaunts and suggesting something of what went on. Briefly, it went like this: Some personable alumnus would guide him through the campus, saying something like "this will be your room, and this is your field house, and this is your training table and this is your coach." The alumnus would chaperone him to fraternity houses and dances and parties over the weekend, giving him the best of good times and only casually reminding him of the economic benefits to be gained.

Wilt has already been to the campuses of Indiana, Michigan and Michigan State. In fact, he was there last year too, and only brought back for a second look this season. As of last December, his friends said Wilt favored Indiana. For one thing, he wants to go out of town. For another, the Indiana alumni have been pointing out to him that Milton Campbell, the high-school football and track wizard from New Jersey, picked the Hoosier school.

But Indiana's edge can be quickly overcome when the full force of Philadelphia's home-town pressure is applied. Wilt may well be prevailed upon to stay at home and play for one of the local schools. Eddie Gottlieb, owner-coach of the Philadelphia Warriors, wants him to, and although he says he has not spoken to Chamberlain yet, there is evidence of his fine hand at work. Gottlieb, understand, doesn't care which Philadelphia school Wilt chooses, just so long as he stays at home. That way, the Warriors get first crack at him in the pro draft four years from now.

A similar high- pressure campaign was used to keep

Tom Gola in Philadelphia. Tom, too, had decided to go out of town to school, and he, too, was talked into the benefits of staying at home.

Meanwhile, the offers continue and Wilt keeps his mouth shut. He could, some people think, even end up at Harvard, which as yet has shown no unusual interest in him. Red Auerbach, coach of the Boston Celtics, who coached Wilt at Kutsher's Country Club, a Catskill Mountain resort, last summer, suggests that he apply for admission at Harvard. "Wilt is an intelligent boy and he should definitely go to school," Red said. "If he went straight into the pros, he'd never get to finish school.

He should go to a good school like Harvard for the education as well as the basketball. I'm not suggesting Harvard because it is in the Celtics' draft area. The kid has to think of the future, when his basketball is over."

Meanwhile, Wilt has remained uncommitted. "I don't intend to decide until after the basketball season," he told us. One thing seems certain. Wilt wants to go to college. He has turned the Globetrotters down cold. He doesn't want the year-round playing, the constant traveling or the bizarre approach to the game. When you talk to him, you get the feeling that the kid senses a need to continue his education.

Usually, in the case of hotshot schoolboy athletes, there is an agent or business adviser who quickly latches on to the boy. But Wilt keeps his own counsel. He listens to everybody but plans to make up his own mind. Or would like to, if people would only let him.

What is it that so many schools see in Chamberlain? His basketball assets are there for all to see. On defense, he stops the other team from scoring. He is more than a goal-tender, though. Overbrook uses a zone defense and Wilt "plays" the basket. He can come out to block a shot before it gets off or he can stay back and slap it away from the rim. He rarely gets charged for goal-tending (touching the rim of the defensive basket) and he fouls infrequently. He plays the backboard like few big men we've ever seen. When a shot is up, he faces the basket—if he can't block the ball—with one hand hovering on either side of it, and jumps. If the ball rebounds left, he grabs it with his left hand. If it bounces to the right, out goes his massive right hand to catch and hold it. Whenever he can use both hands on a rebound, he takes a firm and loud-sounding smack at the ball and comes down hard. It is questionable how college players will react to this, but in high-school ball it is absolutely fearsome.

Once down with a rebound, he knows what to do with the ball. One of the most exciting sights we've seen on a basketball floor is Chamberlain jamming down off a backboard with a ball (when he goes up his elbow is invariably higher than the rim), raring back like a football quarterback and passing the ball one-handed off his ear and across the court to one of his little teammates—usually Marty Hughes, five feet eight inches tall and Wilt's best friend—for a simple layup.

One coach who has been scouting Chamberlain for almost two years said recently that he could find only one flaw in his play, and that not a serious one. "He needs brushing up on defense if he is going to play pro ball some day. We don't allow the zone and he is going to have to come out and take a man. But that is no big problem. Up to now he hasn't had to play defense. Once he moves up to college, he'll learn."

On offense, Wilt carries a heavy arsenal. His best shot is a jump, but because of his height, there is no arc to it. Instead, it is a straight, hard toss that banks in sharply off the backboard. Cecil Mosenson, his coach at Overbrook, explains: "Wilt doesn't take a soft shot. Everything is a line drive. But he has a good eye, a touch and absolute mastery of the backboard. He knows his spots, the angles and just how the ball is going to bounce. Almost every close shot he tries is banked in."

In place of the conventional layup shot, Wilt has a "dunk" shot. Standing flatfooted, he can almost touch the rim with the ball (he misses it by a quarter of an inch). Once he leaves his feet, he jams the ball down the throat of the basket. It touches nothing, not backboard or rim, until it swishes into the nets. Wilt, in fact, leaps so high on most of his layups that (1) he can throw the ball through with one hand and catch it with the other on the way down; (2) he can go up with a ball in each hand and knock both through while in mid-air; and (3) he frequently hurts his forearm against the rim of the basket. He moves and jumps so quickly and slams the ball through the basket so forcefully that, in his follow-through, his arm often smacks into the basket.

Again because of his reach and spring, many of his shots carry only a few inches. This contributes to his amazing shooting average, almost 65 per cent. But it isn't the whole story. Wilt refuses to rely on his close-up shots alone. After his junior year, he felt that he needed a left-handed hook shot to help him move more freely around the bucket. So he began to work on it and developed a good one.

Wilt's hook shots, incidentally, look like layups. He has a gigantic—that's the only word for it—initial stride and can come around the defense in one step. Often, when he gets a pass in the pivot, he holds the ball in one hand as if it were a softball, and, without a dribble, spins around and up in classic hook-shot style. Only, by the time he finishes his arching motion he is up at the basket and lays it in from only a few inches out. Or, when he wants to fool the defense (Overbrook opponents either triple- or quadruple-team him), he'll fake a spin, stick the hand with the ball behind the defenders, while the rest of his body is in front, and toss the ball up underhanded.

Probably as amazing as anything else about this amazing athlete is his stamina. He can run all day. While other big men are usually the first to sit down for a rest, he would be the last, if his coach would let him. But in runaway games, and there have been many, Wilt often plays only one half. In scrimmage, however, he goes all the time. We watched him in a recent two-hour practice against a small-college team. All the other members of the Overbrook squad got to play about equal time. Wilt played straight through, without a break. His stamina, he says, was acquired in the playgrounds when he was a little fellow.

The little fellow was born on August 21, 1936, in Philadelphia of normal size and weight. His parents are of slightly more than average height, his father is five-eight, his mother five nine. "But I had a grandfather, my mother's daddy, who was about seven-two," Wilt says. The other eight children in the family are good-sized. His six sisters are all around five-eight. His older brother, Wilbur, who is 21, is six-four. When Wilt was a youngster, it appeared that he would run about the same, a good-sized fellow but nothing more. Then, when he was 15, he began to shoot up. He grew four inches in three months that summer. By the time he entered Overbrook, he was 6-11, and apparently stopped growing when he was 17. Although not as much as he likes to suggest. If you ask him, Wilt says he is 6-11-1/2. He'll tell you that he has a size 13 foot, a wing span of seven feet two inches and a finger span of 15 inches, but he refuses to be measured. One day at Kutsher's, however, he was taunted by some girls into standing still for the tape. The girls swear he measured seven feet one-half inch.

His sudden growth caused some disturbance at home. His father had to raise all the chandeliers and light fixtures. But nothing could be done about doorways and ceilings, so Wilt still walks around the house in a slight crouch. He sleeps in a regular-sized bed, rolling up into a figure "S" to do it.

Wilt started playing basketball when he was in the seventh grade and made both his school and club teams. He played with boys his own age and size, and did well. Most of his playing was in the Haddington public recreation center, where he would go almost every day to practice. Reports first began to circulate about him when he was 15 and still a little awkward from his sudden growth. People would say, "Did you see that big boy with the long legs walking down Haverford Avenue bouncing a basketball?" Wilt, invariably, was on his way to the recreation center for his daily scrimmage.

He was an immediate sensation when he entered Overbrook in the tenth grade. He led his team to the public school championship, although they lost to West Catholic in the all-city game when four men were put on Wilt. To prepare a defense for Chamberlain, who had been unstoppable all season, the West Catholic coach had a youngster stand on a table placed at the foul line, to simulate Wilt's size, and he had the four players selected to guard Wilt trying to block passes by jumping around the table, waving their hands in his face and generally harassing him. When, in the game, Wilt's unguarded teammates were unable to hit from the outside, West Catholic took a convincing victory.

Last season Overbrook took the championship, the first time in ten years that a public school beat a Catholic school for the city title in Philadelphia. Wilt was high scorer in the city in 1953-54, with a 37.8 average for 12 league games. In a non-league contest, he scored 71 points against Roxborough. He broke all local existing game and season scoring records.

In the city championship game, against South Catholic, Overbrook was prepared for heavy guarding. It had become standard operating procedure by then to drop three men on Wilt. South Catholic did the usual harassing, jumping up and down with their hands constantly in front of his face—but it didn't work. Wilt had learned something about moving around in the bucket and drew 26 fouls. Also, his teammates were hitting from the outside. When their shots were short, he would grab them and drop them in, or carry them along into the basket in one motion. Overbrook won the game, 74-50, with Wilt scoring 32 points.

A change in Wilt's temperament deserves partial credit for his current success. When the publicity first started he was 15 years old and, understandably, he developed a big head. He showboated, didn't try enough, refused to listen and was developing into something of a pest. But when he came back for the 1953-54 season, he was a changed young athlete. He was able to take the publicity in stride. He began helping his teammates, offering them confidence, something he has always had in himself. This season he was made captain and he has taken the assignment seriously. In practice, he doesn't shoot much. Instead, he feeds the ball to the new kids, encouraging them to shoot. He always was good-natured and friendly, but now he has become a leader.

His fellow students are very happy to have him around. He has brought recognition and ballyhoo to the school. When he drives up in his 1947 Oldsmobile ("I bought it, with the money I made bussing tables at Kutsher's"), there is always a gang waiting to greet him. Youngsters on the basketball squad are thrilled to be listed as teammates of his. They sit on the bench during the game, cheering for Wilt, happy when he makes a particularly outstanding basket, proud when he wins a ball game for them. Some of this is even seen in his young coach, who graduated from Overbrook in 1947 and is now only 25 years old.

Despite his height—or maybe because of it—Wilt is an all-around athlete. Although he did not compete in track for Overbrook last spring, Wilt holds several AAU junior records, set when he was 16. Running for the local PAL, he once did 48.8 in the 440. This would be a high-school mark except that only championship meets can be counted as records. His best time in the 880 is 1:58.6, run two summers ago. He has a 15-foot stride and could be one of the best runners ever, says Overbrook track coach Ben Ogden. Although he never competed in the event in high school, he has tossed the 12-pound shot 54 feet eight inches. The high-school record is 51 feet. When he was 15 years old, Wilt says, he once high-jumped six feet five inches. This coming spring he intends to run for Overbrook. If he does, and he can do as well as he did at 16, he might be the next John Woodruff as well as the next George Mikan.

They Make Rules To Stop Bill Russell

Prior to 1955, basketball had not seen anyone quite like Bill Russell. The powerful center led the University of San Francisco to national titles in 1955 and '56—racking up 55 consecutive victories in one stretch—by dominating the backboards and scoring with then unheard of thundering dunks. In the process he caused rule makers to rethink how the game should be played and the rules written. Prior to Russell, basketball's stars were high scorers. But Russell, the 1956 NCAA player of the year, made defense matter. He closed passing lanes, grabbed rebounds and blocked shots with such lethal effect that the NCAA expanded the foul lane from six to twelve feet and began a review of goal-tending. As early as 1955, Russell was earmarked for a standout NBA career, which he delivered with the Boston Celtics, where his hallmark defense would provide the cornerstone for 11 championships from 1957 to 1969.

By Dugal O'Liam
April 1956

IT WAS ALMOST a year ago, with some 11,000 spectators watching the semi-finals of the NCAA basketball tournament in Kansas City, that the furor and debate about Bill Russell, the six-foot, ten-inch center of San Francisco University, reached its peak—a peak that has been maintained right through the entire current season. Playing against Colorado, Russell grabbed a rebound with his back to the basket, leaped above a pack of defenders, and with both hands slammed the ball back over his head and *down* through the basket.

As the ball struck the floor and bounced goal-high, a San Francisco sportswriter shouted to Harry Hanin, scout for the Harlem Globetrotters, "Did you ever see anything like that?"

"No," Hanin said with a gulp, "and I never saw anything like *him*, either."

Hanin's rejoinder was inevitable. Basketball has never had anything like Bill Russell before. He had been working that sort of stunt—and others, like goal-tending—all season long out on the West Coast, but the national limelight was catching his act for the first time. And first-time observers, including scores of college coaches in Kansas City for a rules-committee meeting, were shaken by his performance. Was he a freak? Was his "dunking" unstoppable? Does he do this all the time?

They got their answer the next night when the Dons beat defending champion (and favored) LaSalle, led by all-time All-America Tom Gola, 77-63, to capture the NCAA title. It was a convincing victory, and Russell was so good that the scorers credited six field goals to others although Bill had tipped them in. When asked, their reason was that the shots looked as though they would have gone in without Bill's help. Nor were the scorers the only ones to act against this scourge of the backboards. The college coaches, panicked by the thought that Russell's habit of funnelling wayward shots into the nets could change the game—or at least make San Francisco absolutely unbeatable—decided to legislate against him.

They widened the foul lane from six to 12 feet in what has been called the "Russell Rule."

Dartmouth coach Alvin (Doggie) Julian, a member of the rules committee, said later, "We weren't planning to make any changes in the foul lane. It wasn't a major item on the agenda. But after some of the coaches saw Russell's performance, they got scared and pushed through the 12-foot lane."

Intended to curb Bill's rebounding and tip-ins, the new rule—although generally accepted as a good idea because it opens up the middle—failed to contain the big fellow. USF coach Phil Woolpert predicted at the time that it would only make life more miserable for Bill's opponents. "He's so much the fastest of the big men," Woolpert said, "that now he'll just leave them further behind."

Woolpert was evidently correct. Russell was still able to time his moves and make his tip-ins. The success of Russell and the Dons, and the notice paid to Bill's unusual habits have increased. Rated No. 1 in all the polls right from the start of the season, USF has received national attention in virtually all its games. When, in December, the Dons took a cross-country jaunt that ended up at Christmas time in the Holiday Basketball Festival in Madison Square Garden (which they won), the press concentrated on Russell and produced reams of copy about him. Not all the same copy, though. Watching Big Bill operate, sportswriters and fans alike found they had trouble deciding whether he was genuinely great—or just unusual.

On the pro side of the argument, there is his amazing speed and agility, his jumping talent, his good hook shot and close-in pop shots, his defensive ability, his timing and his downright powerful rebounding. Raps against him include a mediocre outside shot—there is no consistency about it. His greatest offensive skill is jamming the ball down through the basket, and, as one coach watching him in Madison Square Garden said, "There's nothing wrong with scoring your points the easy way, just so long as you score them."

To capitalize on this skill, Frisco has devised a series of dummy plays, which, basically, involve flat shots by teammates, spectacularly tapped or dunked by Russell. For example, if the shot is taken from the corner, it will overshoot the basket, where Russell, able to manhandle a basketball with either hand will leap, grab the ball and—since his hands are now higher than the rim—stuff the ball through.

On defense, Bill will block eight or nine shots a game. Continually, during the course of the Holiday Festival, Bill would leap to block an outside shot or lunge to slap away an attempted driving layup. Against Holy Cross, when he was taken to the outside by All-America Tommy Heinsohn, who has an excellent set shot, Bill was able to block several attempts by the 6-6 Crusader. One writer, watching Russell play Heinsohn (there had been speculation that coach Woolpert wouldn't dare assign Bill to guard Tom, and Woolpert shrewdly refused to deny the report) and seeing how Bill was able to stick with his man on the outside, commented that only someone like Russell could get away with it. A man who shows a tendency to go with a fake, Bill was able to recover in time and, thanks to his exceptional reach, either deflect a shot or prevent a pass underneath. A good example of this occurred in the opening round of the tourney, when a LaSalle player, seeing Russell well in front of him but failing to account for his reach, passed crosscourt only to have Bill reach out and block it. His goaltending technique has become so exasperating, college coaches are now talking about writing in a second "Russell Rule" to contain any successors to his basket-lid defensive maneuvers.

Taking his plus and minus talents together, the current debate about how good Russell is pretty much comes down to this: It is true that Bill is not an all-around basketball player, like Tom Gola or Sihugo Green are. He doesn't have, as they say in the roundball trade, all the tools. But there is no denying his special skills. And, if there must be a last analysis, it can be said that the things Big Bill doesn't do well are things he doesn't have to do.

That goes for college ball only, where his inside work is more than sufficient. It might not be equally true in pro ball, where most players are expected to be able to move away from their normal position at times to maintain full efficiency. Some coaches think his lack of a good outside shot may prevent Bill from being a successful pro. They think he would be a better bet for the Globetrotters, where his special gifts could be exploited to the hilt.

Among those who think Russell is good enough for the pros is the guy who practically made the pros go, George Mikan. "Let's face it," the playing general manager of Minneapolis said after watching Bill, "He's the best ever. He's so good, he scares you." Opinion now is that either the Lakers or the St. Louis Hawks will make him their No. 1 draft choice.

Finishing out what has been a whirlwind collegiate career that will undoubtedly conclude later this month with Russell and Co. defending the NCAA championship, the towering 22 year old has been unlike most giants in that tending and dunking habits. Big Bill looks and behaves like a skillful and confident athlete. Slightly stooped (perhaps an effort to minimize his height and undoubtedly a throwback to more youthful days) Bill's face is solemn and expressionless most of the time. Coming onto the court in his green and yellow sweat suit, he doesn't have the shuffle of Bob (Foothills) Kurland or the pounding might of Mikan. Instead, he moves with the fluidity and control of a true athlete. When he reaches high to catch a pass in one hand and whip it like a baseball to a teammate, he looks graceful and sure. As he goes through his tricks around the backboard, he is in complete control of himself. Coming down with a rebound, he holds tight to the ball, looks carefully before passing out, and moves down court in deceptively fast and amazingly long strides. (Coach Woolpert has a standing rule that his team must delay any offensive play pattern until Russell is down court and in position.)

Bill is, in his long and strong way, a durable player. His shoulders are well formed, the biceps surprisingly full, the forearms hard. His thighs show sturdy sinews, his calves a flowing suppleness. He is neither muscle-bound nor a skinny freak.

On offense, Bill will play the corners as well as in the pivot. He moves well in the deft figure-eight basic pattern of the Dons, and his two-handed overhead passes are vital to Woolpert's planned offense. It is, however, chiefly his defensive play that has made Bill a unanimous All-America choice. Woolpert is a defense-minded coach whose "If you must loaf, loaf on the offense" philosophy has created a defensive team that is more colorful and more popular than the best offensive clubs. Last season, the Dons held their opponents to an average 51.1 points per game, the best defensive record of any major college team, and they are doing almost as well this year.

The main reason for this impressive defensive record is, of course, Russell. He just doesn't allow the opposition much shooting room. "If they can't shoot, they can't score," Woolpert told Bill several years ago, and the happy-go-lucky youngster, working with drive and desire, has executed that principle with exactness and brilliance. A lasting impression of his one-man defensive campaign is that he keeps the opposition off balance. They move into unnatural play patterns to counteract his "balloon barrage," and the inevitable effect is that they are weakened. All season long, the Dons have been better in the second half than in the first half, and the reason seems to be that their defensive tactics have a discouraging effect. In the early rounds of the Holiday Festival, USF did not look good. Woolpert commented that his club's shooting efficiency was way off. Coach Dudey Moore of Duquesne, who had seen the Dons play several times before, said that they were tired and, once rested, would show their real power. Still, they won their games handily. The general explanation for this was that Russell and his indestructible teammate, K.C. Jones, simply wore down the opposition.

Still no ace on offense, in the conventional sense, Bill gets his points, mostly from very close in. He is also a good foul shooter, taking his foul shots with the posturing of the great blue heron, his arms reaching far out in front of his body, one leg dragging well behind. He uses the same flying-crane style on his set shots and, the impression is, he looks as if he expects his shots to miss. Often they do.

Personally, Bill is quiet, a good student, with a

cautious reserve in his speech, a weakness for bedtime snacks and a sincere desire to make good in pro ball, the reason for which is a plan to establish a permanent program for helping underprivileged youngsters. Not that Bill was churchmouse-poor himself; his laborer father always kept his family in dignified comfort. But Bill witnessed critical want and need in his native Louisiana, and later in his Oakland, Cal., neighborhood. He didn't ride to his present heights in any of the familiar subsidized chariots. As a high school player, he received no college bids. And in all his years of high school and college ball, he has yet to play on his own home court. Neither McClymonds High in Oakland nor USF has a gym of its own. While he was at McClymonds, only Hal de Julio, a member of the Dons' 1949 National Invitation Tournament champions (that was the Cinderella team of Rene Herrerias and Don Lofgran) thought much of him. He talked Woolpert into watching Russell, but, although the USF coach was interested, nothing was done. Bill finally went to San Francisco because it had a good business school and was within commuting distance of his home. His arrival there raised little more of a stir than his appearance at McClymonds. This was in the fall of 1949 and Bill, six feet, two inches tall and weighing a feathery 128 pounds, fell over his own and other feet on McClymonds' outdoor court. Coach George Powles, a paternal type, took one look at him and blanched. When, a few minutes later, Russell told him that he figured his destiny was to become the first All-America product from McClymonds, Powles was completely unnerved.

A later, longer and more searching look at Bill, however, convinced Powles that the skinny boy wasn't the type to fall apart. His legs were straight, the shoulders compact and his hands—well, those paws were already startlingly long and flexible. Today Bill's hands measure ten and a half inches from wrist to fingertip, as compared with eight inches for the average adult male.

Powles also thought he saw something in the indomitable spirit of the gangly kid. He took Bill into his own home for indoctrination in morale and attitude, and Bill rewarded him by playing his heart out whenever he was given a chance in the lowliest of scrub games. In his junior year, Bill was third-string center and a sad but determined scapegoat for the cheering section. As time ran out on games in which McClymonds had a safe lead, a derisive chant of "We want Russell" would go up and, fearfully, Powles would send Bill in. He would charge onto the floor and play as if not only the game, but the fate of the Republic, depended on him. The harder he tried, the more he got the raspberries. But even when the catcalls reached the bounds of cruelty, Bill never stopped charging. (During his frosh year at USF, the sight of the traditional green beanie on his head incited digs. This time, Bill resented the jibes and often snapped back.)

By the end of his junior year, Bill was six feet, five inches tall and Powles began to see real promise in him. Out of his personal funds, he bought Bill a membership in a neighborhood athletic club, so he could increase his practice. Bill was now working as a typist before and after school in the McClymonds' offices. His mother had died two years before and the Russell housework devolved upon him. Finishing typing at 5:30 p.m., he would rush home, prepare his father's dinner, and then work out at the club until the director chased him home. Once he arrived with blanket and pillow and asked to sleep on the office floor and lock up when he had finished his practice. He was turned down.

By his senior season, Bill had shot up to six feet, six inches and a summer of hard labor and intensive gym work had hardened his growing muscles. He became McClymonds' first-string center and was on his way to a school scoring record when a penchant for diligent study tripped him up. Instead of finishing his first good season, he was graduated at mid-year, four months ahead of his class.

USF freshman coach Ross Guidice found six feet, eight inches and 195 pounds of Russell on a mediocre squad in 1952. But when he saw Bill jump straight into the air as high as his knees half a dozen times, Guidice told Woolpert he had the new Mikan. Woolpert took one look and right there began building his 1955 champions around Bill.

Those who saw Russell's varsity debut in 1953 in which he faced California's All-Coast Bob McKeen won't soon forget it. Now six feet, nine inches tall and weighing 200 pounds, he scored 23 points to McKeen's 14, dominated the backboards, and blocked 13 shots, eight of them by McKeen. Injuries to key men held the Dons to an indifferent season, however, and Bill entered his junior year little known outside San Francisco. The Northwest had its seven-foot, three-inch Swede Halbrook (Oregon State), the Midwest its Don Schlundt (Indiana), and the South its Dick Hemric (Wake Forest). In the East, Russell simply was ignored. So long as Gola was playing college basketball, the eastern seaboard wasn't much interested in other stars.

The Dons won their first two games easily with Bill establishing a new USF record of 39 points in the opener.

Then came the first of two games with UCLA. Their 47-40 loss was to be the Dons' only defeat of the season. Russell scored only 15 points, but blocked so many shots that a flabbergasted radio announcer said, "This is like a one-man volleyball game."

A week later, the jeers which had taunted Bill before turned into a stirring ovation. With ten minutes left to play in the return game against UCLA in San Francisco, he left the floor with 28 points, 21 rebounds, and 15 blocked field-goal attempts. The Dons were ahead, 52-29, in a game they won, 56-44, and the cheers for Russell lasted for five minutes.

In the All-College tournament at Oklahoma City, USF jumped from 17th place in the national rankings to seventh. Bill was named the tournament's most valuable player, but more important was the record he set for clean play. In four games, beginning with UCLA and ending with Oklahoma City in the tournament semi-finals, he had committed a total of exactly one foul. It was typical of Bill's defensive skills. He never fouled out and averaged only two personals per game.

He also showed a talent for clutch performances. Against Santa Clara, the Dons behind 14 points at half-time, he scored 14 points in four minutes to give USF a lead it never lost. Against Stanford he made 23 points in less than 30 minutes and, at one point, left his feet at the foul line to block a sure layup. Stanford coach Howie Dallmar explained wryly after the game that the Indians had employed three defenses—the zone, man-to-man and panic. None deterred Bill. "He plays at seven-foot, ten," Dallmar, an old pro, said. "He can jump higher than any man in basketball. Mikan would get four field goals a game off Bill. He might get the ball, but he just wouldn't get the shots."

Russell's first crack at a man his own size was against Swede Halbrook, five inches taller and 40 pounds heavier. What happened in that USF-Oregon State battle in the regional NCAA finals has become West Coast basketball legend. Bill scored 29 points, Halbrook 18. With 30 seconds left to play, Oregon State was behind, 57-56, and had possession of the ball out of bounds. Russell blocked a shot, then a held ball had Swede jump against six-foot, one-inch K.C. Jones. Jones' superhuman leap controlled the ball as the game ended. "Did you see that K.C. jump?" Russell exclaimed later. "Man, if I could jump like that!" No one had ever seen Bill so delighted with any feat of his own.

For the NCAA finals at Kansas City, all the talk was about the head-on clash between Russell and 6-7 Gola, mobile, fast, accurate and the best complete basketball player in the college game. When Woolpert assigned Jones to guard Gola, fans and experts alike were startled. But Woolpert wanted Russell free to roam the floor, and figured rugged, high-jumping Jones could handle Gola. Woolpert's strategy worked perfectly. With Gola guarding him, Russell scored 23 points, Gola had 16; Bill took down 22 rebounds, Gola 14. And Big Bill blocked 11 shots. In addition, he set a five-game tournament scoring record with 118 points, bettering Gola's mark of 114 the year before, and was named the tourney's MVP.

"It was a hopeless feeling," LaSalle coach Ken Loeffler said, "seeing Tom going up time and again and not being able to get his hands on the ball."

When the LaSalle game ended, Bill's grim concentration, sometimes mistaken for surliness, dissolved and he leapt about the floor for joy. He pounded the chill, unemotional Woolpert on his lean back and hugged USF regulars and subs with equal fervor. He twice dashed across the floor to shake hands with Gola and he hurdled rows of seats to pump his father's hand and smother his stepmother in an embrace. The following day, he was shown a picture in a news magazine of Loeffler briefing his team for the Don game. Behind the coach was a blackboard listing four Don regulars, their outstanding points and what to do about them. Besides Bill's name, however, appeared only the single word, "Gola." Bill viewed the picture with neither annoyance nor triumph. His eyes popped and his mouth fell open. "Man," he exclaimed, "am I lucky we had good old K.C. around!"

Back in San Francisco, the Russell legend began taking tangible form. Local citizens had touched off a campaign to build a $700,000 gym for the homeless heroes and when the squad debarked at San Francisco Airport, $400,000 already had been pledged.

Bill's eagerness to share his joy with his family in Kansas City was characteristic of the strong bond among the Russells. Charles Russell, Sr., took his wife and two sons to Oakland from Monroe, La., when the wartime shipyards mushroomed in the San Francisco Bay area. He housed them in a neat, five-room apartment where they still live. When, a year after the close of World War II, the first Mrs. Russell died, her last words enjoined her husband to give Bill and Charles, Jr., called Chuck in the family and two years Bill's senior, college educations.

Both sons' athletic ability has helped Charles Russell fulfill the request: Chuck was a football and basketball star in high school and junior college and now, after two years' military service, is enrolled at St. Mary's College in California. In junior high school, Chuck set a school record for the 100-yard dash about which he grew too loquacious to please his father. "Boy," the senior Russell said, "you need another lesson in running before you talk too much."

He led Chuck to a public park and while Bill watched, outran him for a hundred yards while wearing working shoes. "Now," he said, "try to remember that if you have to talk about yourself, talk about something you don't do well."

The incident made a deep impression on Bill and his reluctance to talk of his strong points is no pose. He'll talk willingly about his shortcomings, however, insisting, for example, that he is the poorest shot on the USF team. Asked to give some reasons why he also scores so heavily, he replies: "Four guys who play with me and the luck that made me six feet, nine and five-eighths inches tall."

One of Bill's basketball assets is his ambidexterity. He shoots, passes, dribbles and rebounds with either hand. Back in Monroe, his uncle Robert Russell had ambitions to be a star first baseman in the Negro professional baseball leagues and blamed his failure on the fact he wasn't left-handed. He decided to make Bill a southpaw. If the young boy could develop into a left-handed pitcher, Uncle Bob figured, he might play good enough sandlot ball to earn a scholarship. There was no thought of basketball involved, since a Negro boy's prospects for good high-school basketball training in Monroe were almost nonexistent. Uncle Bob made him eat and pick up things with his left hand; and after a while Bill did become a southpaw—but not in baseball. He forgot that sport soon after coming to Oakland. Chuck started playing basketball first, and when Bill followed him he quickly decided this was his sport.

Not a bad choice, at that. The Globetrotters have not been hiding their keen interest in the big fellow. They want him badly; and some people say they *need* him badly, too. But their chances are shaky. Bill has said he would not want to make his living as a clown. He does hope to make the pros. Only trouble is he also wants to make the Olympic team, and for that you must be a simon-pure amateur. His Olympic ambitions are not only in basketball, either. As a sometime high jumper, he has already cleared six feet, eight inches, and Dink Templeton, the gravel-voiced West Coast track sage, has pronounced Bill potentially the greatest high jumper in history. "Give him a year to work on his form," Templeton says, "and he'll do seven feet with his hands in his pockets."

Since Bill can also run the 440 in 49.6, he figures to combine these track talents and train for the 400-meter hurdles, too. And he just might make it, too—if he really makes the try. As the only college guest at President Eisenhower's conference with the country's leading athletes, Bill promised Ike he would stay an amateur until after the Olympics. The pros are already waving reasonably fat checks in front of him, but to try to qualify for the trip to Melbourne in November, Bill will have to pass up signing with the NBA until next year. Now that his astonishing basketball skills have been pretty well accepted throughout the country, the next interesting question about Bill Russell is which way will he turn— and how will he go?

Doak Walker:
The Eternal Hero

Many had predicted a short NFL career for Doak Walker. At just 168 pounds when he joined the Detroit Lions in 1950, there was a consensus that the Heisman winner from SMU would be carted into retirement on a stretcher soon after his debut. As it turned out, Walker's career was indeed relatively brief. But when he retired in 1955, after leading the NFL in scoring, it wasn't on a stretcher. The versatile halfback sprinted from the field to an eventual home in the Hall of Fame. In this retrospective look at Walker, Arnold Hano marvels at the skill and grit of a player who led the NFL in scoring in his rookie season—in one game against Green Bay, Walker scored all Detroit's points in a 24-21 win—and who led the Lions to two championships before his surprising decision to retire at the peak of his career.

BY ARNOLD HANO
OCTOBER 1969

"The game . . . was played from three of a snappy exhilarating afternoon far into the crisp autumnal twilight, and Amory at quarterback, exhorting in wild despair, making impossible tackles, calling signals in a voice that had diminished to a hoarse, furious whisper, yet found time to revel in the blood-stained bandage around his head, and the straining, glorious heroism of plunging, crashing bodies and *aching limbs. For those minutes, courage flowed like wine out of the November dusk, and he was the eternal hero, one with the sea-rover on the prow of a Norse galley, one with Roland and Horatius . . ."*

—*F. Scott Fitzgerald:* This Side of Paradise

DOAK WALKER WORE no bloodstained bandage around his head. He wore the blood-red helmet of Southern Methodist University. Change nothing else in the above and you have not the fictional hero, Amory Blaine, but the real-life hero, Ewell Doak Walker, Jr. On those November afternoons in the postwar 1940s, Doak Walker became the eternal hero. And courage flowed like wine.

For three years, Doak Walker was an All-American; fewer than a handful of athletes in all of football's hundred years can make such a claim. More, he was a true All-American, if we look at the term we are using. Surely it is not enough just to run, pass, block, tackle, receive, punt, placekick, and call signals, as Doak Walker did. That's the "All" part of All-American. But what about the "American?" Is the physical man all we ask of in an American? Nonsense. Doak Walker had the courage we admire in our heroes. He also had the modesty and prudence that make heroism acceptable, and not so much bluster. He comported himself like a man—fair, honorable, just. He kept his character as strong as his muscles, as untainted as his blood. He believed in simple food; at college he never tasted liquor (or, rather, he tasted it once and hated it). He never smoked. He preached and practiced moderation. At the peak of his college career, he received 200 to 300 fan letters a week. Doak Walker answered them all himself.

He says, today, "They wrote to me. It would have been rude not to answer." A newsweekly magazine once wrote how Walker dumped fan mail, unread, into a wastebasket. An outright lie. How did Doak Walker feel when people lied about him? "The magazine had to write something. No player was blessed with fairer, finer, more honest press coverage than I was."

Lest you think we have magnified Doak Walker into something that never was, permit me to highlight a few of Walker's moments as a football player. He enrolled at SMU in mid-October of 1945. With three days' practice, he made the varsity football team—as a freshman—and on Saturday played his first football game, against Bobby Layne and Texas U. Texas was the powerhouse of the Southwest Conference, SMU the doormat. Texas edged SMU that day, 12-7. Walker played Layne to a standstill, each man passing for a touchdown, each man intercepting the other's pass on the goal line to thwart a score. SMU went on to win its three remaining league games, and Doak Walker made the All-Conference team, second in the balloting only to Layne. He was so good so quickly, he quarterbacked the West in the annual East-West Shrine game on January 1, 1946, Doak Walker's 19th birthday. He was still a freshman. He passed for his team's only touchdown; the game ended 6-6.

For the next three years at college, no halfback in the nation was better. He ran, he passed (he had a higher percentage of pass completions than Bobby Layne), he caught passes, he blocked savagely. He played defense, guarding his goal like Horatius at the bridge. Texans still talk about the 1947 TCU-SMU contest, how TCU went ahead, 19-13, with less than a minute to play, and how tackle Harold Kilman taunted Walker with, "Well,

Doak, what are you going to do now?"

"We're going to score again," Walker replied. He had already ripped off runs of 80, 61 and 56 yards. Now he took the kickoff, and ran it back 56 yards, moving along the sideline like a slithering ghost. On that 56-yard gallop, as TCU tacklers moved in on Walker, Doak took time to yell to coach Matty Bell, as he glided by the Southern Methodist bench, "Send Johnson in now."

Bell—who used to say, "Having Doak in the game was like having a coach on the field,"—obediently sent in Gil Johnson, and the clutch passer pitched a ball to Walker, who made a miraculous catch on the nine. With the whole defense now keyed on Walker, Johnson tossed to Sid Halliday in the end zone, for the tying score. Fortunately for our credulity, Walker missed the extra point. He was, after all, human, though you could not have so asserted from his stats in that game—471 yards gained by running and passing.

On the streets of Dallas or Fort Worth, in 1947 and '48, Doak Walker was Jim Bowie and Sam Houston, Davey O'Brien and Sam Baugh. Robert B. Cullum, president of Dallas's Salesmanship Club, would say at banquets: "Because we have so many visitors present we will dispense with the usual Dallas custom of standing at attention and holding hands over the heart whenever Doak's name is mentioned."

He was two things: the shy kid next door, and a Texas god. Once, Rice lineman Gerald Weatherly had rushed at Walker as Doak ran the ball out of bounds. Though Walker stopped, Weatherly kept coming, unable to stem his momentum. He hit Walker a blindside blow that hurled the young man against a wheelchair, knocking him senseless. SMU lost the game. When it was over,

Walker went to the Rice dressing room, to congratulate the victors, and to tell big Weatherly he knew the collision hadn't been intentional.

No, he was not stupid. He knew the score. A year later he would say to another Rice player, "Just how big was that pot you guys had for me last fall?" Football wasn't all romance. Players put up money, the jackpot to go to the guy who knocked a rival star out of commission. The Rice player said he didn't know there'd been such a pot, and Walker grinned: "I just wanted to know how much you guys figured I was worth."

Not stupid. But you don't cry. The head goes higher, you take your licks like a man. Yet a theme recurs. Walker was a Texan, and Texans know all about money. Slice a Texan's wrist, and the arteries gush oil, not blood.

Walker was, and is, human. Today, 42 years old this New Year's Day, his sandy hair now darkened, touches of grey at the sideburns, his body has thickened. He says he weighs 15-20 pounds over his playing weight of 168, but it looks closer to 30 pounds. He married his college sweetheart, but they divorced. At SMU he often went around barefoot; today he wears splendidly gold-green sports jackets and soft white Texan shoes. He never drank in college, but he had his occasional beer in the pros, and today he will drink cocktails or beer or anything. Though he loves the pro game and goes to games whenever he can, and though he lives in suburban Detroit, he does not particularly root for the Lions, for whom he played his six years in the pros. "They don't pay me anymore," he says. "When I had an interest—a money interest—it was different."

I said he lives in suburban Detroit. He also keeps a home in Steamboat Springs, Colorado, and he spends much time in Denver, Los Angeles and New York. "I live in the iron bird," he says, looking at the sky. He is an enormously successful salesman, and when he talks about his old SMU teammates, he says, "A whole bunch of those boys are millionaires today." Walker won't say how much he earns, but one suspects he is, or is about to be, one of those millionaires.

Money moves Doak Walker as it does the rest of us. He is human.

Or so we have to remind ourselves. He graduated from SMU and joined the Detroit Lions, too small at 168 pounds to make good in the pros. So everybody said. In his rookie season, 1950, he led the league in scoring, with 128 points. He led the league again in 1955, his final season. For four seasons he was All-League. He remains, today, the highest scorer in Lion history. During his six seasons, Detroit played in three world title games, and won two of them.

He was unique. He quit football, 28 years old, at the peak of his talent. He said, later, "I wanted to get out while I had all my teeth and both my knees." And he said, the other afternoon in Denver, where he had just played nine holes of golf (in 38 strokes), "Football was fun. I loved it. Today, with TV, there is too much pressure on players, on coaches, on teams. You have to win. Too much money is involved. You must produce or else. It takes the fun out of the game. My father used to say— 'Remember, it's only a game.'"

Doak Walker came to football just as World War II was ending, and America was entering her moneyed era. He became, for three years, the last great romantic hero of an era soon spent. He took us out of what F. Scott Fitzgerald once called "the deep locker rooms of the earth" and brought us into the golden stadiums, where courage flowed before us like wine. Football remained, for those brief years, our most romantic pastime.

Today, the press conference is a more natural arena for our athletes than the football stadium. Today, Horatius holds them off at the bridge, while his agent sells the exploit to *Life*. If the price isn't right, t'hell with the bridge. We have burned Horatius's bridges behind us.

So we remember Doak Walker, the eternal hero, to rebuild those bridges with our past. Yes, Doak Walker knew all about money, but he played for something else, and we search to recall what it was.

Ewell Doak Walker, Jr., was born on January 1, 1927, the year of Ruth's 60 homers, of the Dempsey-Tunney Long Count, and of the rebirth of a lesser athlete.

Ewell Doak Walker, father of the New Year's infant, school teacher and high-school football coach, had once played football at Austin College, in Sherman, Texas. Few people remembered Ewell Walker had wanted to be a star. "The fact that he wasn't," said Texas sportswriter Bill Rives, "disturbs his spirit."

So Ewell Walker set out to mold his son into the player he'd wanted to be. The story has it that when asked at Doak's birth what he wanted his son to be—President?—Ewell Walker replied: "No. He's going to be an All-American."

Ewell shoved regulation footballs against the boy's belly when Doak was two. "Why, he's too little to handle footballs that big," Doak's mother said. "He might as well get used to it now," Ewell answered. By six, Doak Walker could dropkick over the clothesline.

The Walkers sent the boy to camp every summer, and

Doak became adept at all sports. The outdoors became his milieu. Today when you ask Doak Walker how he'd feel in an office job, tied to a desk from nine to five, he says, "I wouldn't take the job. I like the great outdoors too much. I must move about."

He grew strong, capable of throwing and catching a ball, maintaining his balance, linking mind to muscle. He thickened at shoulders, neck, chest and upper arms. His upper legs were heavy, rockhard with muscle. Still, at his physical peak, he stood less than 5-11, and weighed 168 pounds.

For all the molding by his father, some of it came from within. One day Doak arrived an hour late after an errand for his mother. His mother punished him by keeping him in that day. A week later, the boy came home, wearing a new pair of sneakers.

"Where did you get those?" his mother asked.

"Remember when I came home late?" he said. "I'd passed a store window on the way back that day. There was a leopard skin hanging there, and a sign that anyone who guessed the number of spots would get the shoes."

"But does it take an hour to make a guess?" his mother wanted to know.

"I didn't guess," the boy said. "I counted every spot."

Doak and his father often played chess together. On occasions Doak would beat his father. Win or lose, the boy transferred the lessons of chess to the football field. "Football," Doak Walker says today, "is a chess game. You must get your opponent out of position. When you have two strong men, with basically the same abilities, the man who makes fewer mental mistakes will win."

Maneuvering other people meant survival, later. "I never got hit a solid shot," Doak Walker says, and if it is hyperbole, memory misted by time, it isn't gross. When Walker played, he never seemed to run at a man, dead on. Always he ran at an angle to the defense, so you seldom had a clean shot at him. His size, he thinks, was an asset. "A smaller man always should be able to move a bigger man."

He turned his chess mind to football, particularly when he joined the pros in 1950. You ask him today—how did he possibly succeed in a sport where far greater size and strength have always been deemed absolute requisites?

"I had natural ability and agility," he says. Gently he refutes the notion he wasn't strong enough. "I began as a blocking back. I had strong legs, shoulders, arms. I had a great background. Rusty Russell, who coached me in high school and later at SMU, was a true student of the game." But then he gets down to it. "I would study game films, see how the line moved, how the linebacker covered his weakness."

But doesn't everybody study game films?

Quickly: "Not the way I did." And you picture the boy's patient mind counting every leopard spot or studying his father's pawns and bishops, and plotting his next move and the one beyond that.

But we have leaped in time. He took his budding skills to Highland Park High, in Dallas, where he played under Rusty Russell, and with a big blond laughing youngster named Bobby Layne, one year ahead of Doak. The two became fast friends. They played at Highland Park together, they joined the maritime service together, they played against each other in the Southwest Conference, and again together with the Lions.

Not that Walker needed Layne; his greatness (and Layne's) would develop independently. At Highland

Park, in his senior year (after Layne had graduated), Walker lettered in five sports, and during his high-school career, acquired more letters (12) and captaincies than any student in the school's history.

He joined Bobby Layne in the maritime service. Layne came out to resume his college career at Texas U., while Walker was torn between Texas and hometown SMU. The boys attended an SMU-Tulane game early in 1945. Tulane whipped SMU, and Layne said, "Why don't you go to Texas with me? We'll be playing on a good team, not a bunch of ragknots."

But Doak's father pointed out the value of playing in front of friends, and Rusty Russell, the boy's former coach at Highland Park and now assistant coach at SMU, came by to apply more pressure. Walker finally agreed, and three days after he'd enrolled, he became the team's No. 1 back.

Walker spent the next season in the Army, and returned in 1947 for the full three years remaining of his varsity eligibility. These were the glory years at SMU; for two years, the Mustangs won the Conference and went to the Cotton Bowl. For three years running, they beat arch foe Texas. In 1948, Walker became the first junior to win the Heisman Trophy. The year before, as a soph, he'd finished third. The great days became commonplace.

On January 1, 1948, SMU played heavily favored and undefeated Penn State in the Cotton Bowl. Penn State boasted the finest defense in the nation. SMU scored the second time it had the ball. Walker ran for 15 yards, and then threw a 50-yard bomb to Paul Page, who caught the ball on the 13 and ran it in. Later, Walker cracked over his right tackle for a second score. Penn State also scored twice, and the game ended, 13-13.

The next year, in the Cotton Bowl as 69,000 looked on, SMU whipped favored Oregon, 21-13. Walker completed six of ten passes, quick-kicked 80 yards to the half-foot line, threw a block that sprang Kyle Rote to the two, where Doak then carried it over. Oregon coach Jim Aiken shook his head. "What can you say? He was the works; the greatest I've ever seen." Oregon's own star was Norm Van Brocklin. On that day, Walker passed as well as Van Brocklin.

But recounting his heroic deeds, we miss the flavor of the man. Bill Rives once wrote: "The nation fell in love with this boy as it learned bit by bit of his strong character, his good sportsmanship, his wholesome life." Coach Bell said: "You get an indication of what sort of boy he is when you know there isn't a single player on the squad who is jealous of him . . . He is one of the finest kids I ever knew."

His fame spread. *SPORT* magazine put his face on its cover, and so did *Life*. A racehorse was named O.K. Doak; the Lions Club of Dallas named him the city's No. 1 citizen. In his freshman year at SMU, students voted him the outstanding young man on campus. The Dallas junior chamber of commerce voted him the city's leading young citizen. He was chosen one of the outstanding Presbyterians of 1949. He met a honey-haired coed, Norma Peterson, who later became queen of the Drake Relays and yearbook queen at SMU. They fell in love and married in 1950. The world lay at his feet.

He came to the pros, where a man his size seldom lasts a week into training camp. He lasted six years, the greatest player in Detroit Lion history, and we include Whizzer White, Dutch Clark, Bill Dudley and Bobby Layne.

On November 19, 1950—his rookie season—Walker

scored all the Lions' points in a 24-21 win over Green Bay. Four days later, the Lions beat the New York Yanks, 49-14, rolling up what was then the biggest Detroit score of all time. New York writer Rud Rennie turned lyrically fey: ". . . the most dazzling ball-carrier on the field was Walker. His change of pace and his faking were beautiful to see. He ran, he caught passes, he punted . . . and he kicked all seven points after touchdown. He changes a shoe every time he kicks. He was worn out changing shoes."

But he was human. That 1950 Lion club ended up six-and-six, under coach Bo McMillin. The players felt it should have been better. They went to the Lion owners and asked for McMillin's scalp. They got it. Walker took part in the rebellion. "We felt Bo had not been getting the full potential out of the club. He ran the team by himself. He had two great assistants, Buddy Parker and George Wilson. He never used them." Shortly after McMillin was fired he died of cancer. Walker says today: "That is why Bo acted the way he did. He was sick then, and nobody knew it."

So Doak Walker looked out for himself. He opened up the southwest to the pros. Detroit began to barnstorm through Texas before each NFL season. Walker received a percentage of the gate for those Texas games. He was worth it. Sometimes it cost him. In 1952, the Lions played three exhibitions in Texas in 11 days; Walker earned $7000, but the Texas heat drained away his strength, and he weighed just 149 pounds when the season opened against San Francisco. Dehydrated and weak, he strained a muscle on an open-field block, and never recovered the rest of 1952. He was still not in shape when Detroit played Cleveland for the world title in December, but no matter. He played. With the Lions leading 7-0 in the third quarter of a bristling game, Walker took a handoff from Layne, darted through a hole between guard and tackle, and exploded for 67 yards and a touchdown. The Lions went on to win, 17-7.

He was the best, in college and in the pros, and today, Doak Walker, married once again, with four children by his first marriage, is a successful man in the business world. He is the vice president, in charge of corporate sales, for the nation's largest electrical contractors, Fischbach & Moore. Success marks him. When he talks about football today, he says, "College football was really just a steppingstone, for the opportunity to play pro ball. It was a phase of maturing my skills, a place to correct mistakes, to gain the knowledge to take me to the next level of football."

But he also says, "Football was very important to me, the only thing in my life." Because it was so important, it developed a dynamics of its own, and though Doak Walker always knew where he was going, sometimes he couldn't have changed directions had he wanted. His wife Norma wanted Doak to quit football long before he did. An athletic career does not make for what the rest of us call a "normal" family life. You are away too much. You lead a monastic existence in training camps. You travel, you train, you play. All else is made to yield to the single objective, the Saturday or Sunday game. Doak Walker will not say football wrecked his first marriage, but he won't say it didn't. One suspects it played a role. The Walkers divorced. Doak met Skeeter Werner, sister of the late Bud Werner, one of America's premier skiers who was killed in an avalanche a few years ago. Skeeter Werner skied on the American Olympic team of 1956. Her life is as tuned to the outdoors, to sports, to play, as is Doak's. They married May 19, 1969.

But our story is not The Newlywed Game. It is football. Walker left the pro ranks in 1955, but he discovered an old truth. You can take Doak Walker out of football, but you can't take football out of Doak Walker. Not easily, anyway. Walker thought he wouldn't miss football, but he found his life had a void.

"I couldn't watch a game," he recalls today. "I didn't go to a game for a couple of years. My hands would sweat at the thought. I couldn't even watch it on TV."

In 1957, nearly two years after he had retired, Doak Walker began to work out in Boulder, Colorado, tossing a football back and forth. Word leaked out to the Lions. Coach Buddy Parker phoned Walker. "I understand you're working out," the coach said. "How'd you like to play ball again?"

Walker says: "It rang bells."

He went to camp. "I figured I'd give it five or six days. I'd get my fanny kicked off, and that would be that. It would be out of my system."

He worked out for a few days, and then the Lions held their first scrimmage. "You never have a good day that first scrimmage," Walker says. "Your timing is shot. You're not in shape."

So Doak Walker, six months past his 30th birthday, out of the game a full season plus, stood in the Lion backfield again, expecting only the worst.

He had a fantastic day. He ripped off long runs. He ran immaculate patterns and caught passes for long gains. He reached for whatever magic lay in his bones, and it all responded, on cue.

That night, lying on his back in a bunk at camp, Doak Walker said to himself: "What in the world are you doing here?"

He got up, at midnight, and left the Detroit camp.

That was that. Why had he done it? He isn't sure. "I let my enthusiasm run away," he says today, but it must be more. He had to prove to himself that he could still play. He had unfinished business. He had tried to retire from football, but football had not been ready. The game has a life of its own. He had to have his last hurrah. He had it. He closed the book. He found he could go to games again. His hands didn't get wet.

Perhaps there is even more. Heroes, in our foolish romantic insistence, do not change. Old soldiers never die. Great football players, especially of those days now past, remain as they always were, making impossible tackles and more impossible runs and catches. In a single scrimmage, Doak Walker proved how right we are to believe such foolishness. Still, reality intrudes on romance, in this practical, grubby world of ours. So I asked him, the other afternoon, "Do you think, in your prime, you could have played with today's pros?" my mind picturing the smallish Walker up against Deacon Jones, Bob Lilly, Dick Butkus, and other beasts of the field.

His eyes glinted. He seemed amused. "Oh, yes," he said. "I could play."

Why not? He was Doak Walker, and Doak Walker was the best.

Richard, Beliveau And The '55 Canadiens

In Montreal, where hockey reigns supreme, 1955 is the year the fans held a riot and the Canadiens came out fighting. The riot occurred in March outside the Montreal Forum after superstar Maurice "Rocket" Richard was suspended for the season for his part in an on-ice brawl. The suspension cost Richard the league scoring title and the Canadiens the Stanley Cup. It also cost the city of Montreal untold thousands of dollars in cleanup costs. But the most lasting effect of the riot, as Josh Greenfeld detailed a decade later, was that it put the fight back into a Canadiens franchise that had grown soft in the 1950s. Beginning in the autumn of '55, the team of Richard, Beliveau, Geoffrion, Harvey and Plante, under the direction of new coach Toe Blake, went on a tear that would bring Montreal an unprecedented five consecutive championships and everlasting fame as the Flying Frenchmen.

BY JOSH GREENFELD
MAY 1966

THEY HAD THE ROCKET and the Pocket and the Boom; they had Dickie Moore and Doug Harvey; they had Jake the Snake and *Le Gros Bill* and, as *Instructeur*, Toe Blake. They were the largest collection of superstars ever assembled on a single team. They played the most colorful hockey the league had ever seen. They were the first of five Canadien clubs to come charging out of Montreal in the Fifties to win an unparalleled five Stanley Cups in succession. They were the 1955-56 Canadiens—if not the greatest hockey team of all time, certainly the most explosive one.

"I remember the first practices I had with those fellows," Toe Blake reminisced recently in his Montreal Forum office. "I was glad I was as young as I was. Otherwise, I would have been killed. All those great shots. The puck was flying around with such speed I thought I was in a shooting gallery."

So, too, did the NHL goalies that season. Four of the top seven scorers were Canadiens. Jean Beliveau led the league with 88 points to win the Art Ross Trophy; Maurice Richard was third (71 points), Bert Olmstead fourth (70 points), and Boom Boom Geoffrion seventh (62 points). Four individual members placed on the league All-Star Team: Beliveau, Maurice Richard, Harvey and Plante; two men made the second team: Olmstead and Tom Johnson. Goalie Jacques Plante won the Vezina Trophy with a GAPG (Goals against per game) average of 1.86; Doug Harvey took the James Norris Trophy as the league's best defenseman; Beliveau was awarded the Hart Trophy as the league's most valuable player. And the '55-56 Canadiens ran away with the NHL championship by a bulge of 24 points or 12 games; winning a record-making 45 games while losing 15 and tying 10 for 100 points, one point below the season record set by the '50-51 Red Wings.

But statistics and individual awards tell only a small part of the story; for mostly they were a team, a smoothly functioning cohesive unit. "I'm lucky I was a member of that team," recalls Beliveau modestly. "We had everything. We had great scoring, we had great checking, we had great goaltending. And we had great blending: What I mean is sometimes a team is too old or a team is too young. We had the right combination of experienced veterans and good young rookies. And we had great team spirit. No question about that."

Red Fisher, Montreal *Star* sports columnist, echoes that observation: "You know, it's no secret that after a game most hockey players around the league like to have a beer or two to unwind. Usually you see them drift out of the dressing rooms in twos and threes, little groups going their separate ways. But not that club. After a game they'd all go out together. You'd walk into a tavern and see 15, 16 of them sitting around one big table. Maybe the Rocket wouldn't be there or Jake Plante—they were loners—but otherwise, the whole team would always be together, always doing everything together. I never saw another team that stuck so close together off the ice."

On the ice the most dramatic example of the '55-56 Canadiens in action came in their execution of the power play—the deadliest five-man charge in the history of hockey. Once they brought the puck across center ice, Harvey and Geoffrion would station themselves at the "points," the opposite ends of the shorthanded rival's blue line. There, they would act as playmakers or feeders as they passed the puck back and forth, maneuvering for a clear shot or whip passes to one of the three onrushing forwards, Beliveau, Richard or Olmstead, who were swarming about the net, setting up screens as they did so.

All teams, of course, have power plays, but what made that of the '55-56 Canadiens so devastating were the special individual talents acting in concert. Harvey could thread-needle a pass through any defense onto the waiting sticks of Beliveau or Richard, two superb close-up shots. Olmstead could scoot and retrieve, dig a puck out of any corner and get it back into action. And Geoffrion had developed the long slapshot to perfection. Often Montreal would draw the defense to one side, then whisk the puck to Geoffrion, storming in from his right point, who would then let loose a 40-foot shot of bee-line accuracy.

In fact, so great was their power play—they scored over *25 percent* of their goals on it—the league instituted a rule change the following season. Thereafter, the scoring of a goal terminated a minor penalty.

But the most important achievement of the '55-56 Canadiens did not take place in the rule book; it took place on the ice in the Stanley Cup finals. There, by whipping the Detroit Red Wings in five games, they set the pattern for a dynasty that was to completely dominate the league for the rest of the decade.

Much has been written about the Montreal mystique in hockey and most of it is true. Yet nothing can really explain the unique electric excitement, the super-charged emotion, the raw-nerved tension which surrounds a Canadiens hockey team; there simply isn't an analogy in sports for it. Montrealers do not merely love their Canadiens, do not just adore them; they *need* them. And this need finds expression in an inordinately strong desire to win.

Winning in hockey, of course, means only one thing—the Stanley Cup.

In the early 1950s the Canadiens were like a team of destiny—except their destiny was continually eluding them. Each season they would reach the Stanley Cup finals; and each season they would skate away empty handed. These were the high-flying years of the Red Wings—from 1948-1949 to 1954-55 the Red Wings won seven consecutive NHL championships, and four Stanley Cups—and a situation which under any conditions, to say the least, would have been unbearable to Canadiens partisans was gradually becoming more and more impossible.

In 1952-1953, the Canadiens did sip champagne from the Stanley Cup by turning back a hustling Boston Bruin team that had slipped by the Red Wings. Now the Canadiens fans reckoned that a new era had arrived. It hadn't. The next season they finished seven points behind Detroit in the final NHL standings, and lost to the Red Wings in the Stanley Cup finals.

So 1954-1955 *had* to be the season. But it wasn't. It wasn't, but an incident that occurred in Boston on March 13, 1955, may have set the scene for the following year.

Maurice Richard, naturally, was the focal point. After receiving a scalp cut from high-sticking Hal Laycoe that would require eight stitches, an enraged Richard went after Laycoe. In the ensuing melee the Rocket snapped his stick into splinters across Laycoe's back and brought his fist to bear against the face of official Cliff Thompson. Thompson filed the report to the league office and President Clarence Campbell took stern action. He suspended Richard for the balance of the season.

Montreal was left in a state of trembling shock. It was as if suddenly the carpet had been pulled out from under an entire city. For here was the beloved Richard being deprived of the best opportunity he had enjoyed during his long career to win the scoring race, the single honor that had eluded him. With the season drawing to a close it seemed evident that he would be the league leader, with teammates Bernie Geoffrion and Jean Beliveau finishing behind him. It had also seemed evident that the team as a whole would finish four points ahead of the Red Wings, thereby not only breaking the six-year Detroit reign as NHL champions, but also giving the Canadiens the crucial extra home game in the Stanley Cup finals.

The Canadiens had but three remaining games: two against the Red Wings and one against the Rangers. The first of their meetings with Detroit was on March 17, St. Patrick's Night, at the Forum. Tension gripped the air before the game even began; but the game was never finished.

A Forum crowd on the best of nights can be an ugly animal; on this night it was like a snarling beast. Over 200 policemen inside the arena were unable to maintain order. That was not enough when Clarence Campbell entered the Forum midway in the first period, the Canadiens already behind. There was a shower of eggs, peanuts, programs, even overshoes.

A fan came over and slugged Campbell and then a smoke bomb exploded. Campbell immediately awarded the game to the Red Wings on a forfeit and the rioting spilled out onto the street.

It was an ugly riot as all riots are, one of the worst riots in Montreal's history. Shots of rifle fire ringed the air. The mob, like a herd of cattle, stampeded down rue de Ste. Catherine up-ending cars, breaking windows, looting stores, roughing up passersby. Over $100,000 worth of private property was damaged, and more than 100 people were arrested. Finally, Maurice Richard had

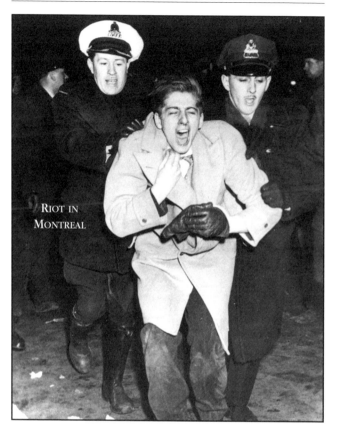

RIOT IN
MONTREAL

to take to the air.

Speaking over the radio in French, then English, Richard pleaded for calm, for a return to order. "I will take my punishment," he said, "and come back next year to help the club and the younger players win the Cup."

He was true to his word. The Canadiens lost the league championship and lost the Stanley Cup to Detroit. But a dynasty was born.

Some teams are born with greatness, others achieve greatness, and the simple chemistry that makes for the formation of a great team is one of the eternal fascinations of sports.

The '55-56 Canadiens present an object lesson, an almost laboratory-controlled example of the intrinsic merit of two of the more commonly advanced "great team" theory formulas. For what distinguished the '55-56 Canadiens most from their tragedy prone forerunners—in addition to the actual emotional stimulus of the riot—was a change in *leadership* and a change in *attitude*.

The leadership change came first. On June 8, 1955, before a Canadian-wide television and radio hook-up, Toe Blake was officially signed as new coach, replacing Dick Irvin who was moving over to coach the Chicago Black Hawks after 15 years at Montreal. Frank Selke, the Canadien General Manager, had decided the club needed a coach who could handle the players rather than spur them, someone who could pacify as well as prod. For it had been decided that Irvin too often fanned the fires that burned in the tempestuous Richard instead of banking them, which was a little like pouring oil upon troubled gasoline.

Blake had a special relationship with Richard. Having played on the same line with the Rocket—the famed Punch Line of Richard, Blake and Elmer Lach—he understood the exceptional nature of the remarkable Richard. And the Rocket knew that. Shortly after the announcement of Blake's hiring, Richard assured Selke that he approved of the appointment. "We all love the old Lamplighter," he told Selke. "We'll give him every ounce we've got."

Meanwhile, Blake and Selke were trying to give the

Rocket all they had by way of a tranquilizing program. Reckoning that a subdued Rocket was better than a suspended one, they gave him de-pep talks long before the season began. They pointed out to him that he was 35 years old, that he did not have to carry the emotional burden of victory alone, that he still would be treated with sufficient respect by the other players around the league even if he went a little easier on the rough-house, and that the important thing was not one game, not one fight, but to lead the team to a Stanley Cup victory.

Toe Blake vividly remembers that first training camp at Verdun in his charge. "I could see from the start we would have good harmony on the club. The boys were greatly disappointed with the way they'd finished the last two years. One year a bad goal beat them, the next year a bad fuss. They were determined they were not going to let anything beat them this time, least of all themselves.

"I was nervous. I felt I had to produce with a club like that. So much potential. And it was a big test for me. But the Rocket went out of his way to help me. So did Kenny Mosdell and Floyd Curry and Butch Bouchard. You know, sometimes it's awful hard to coach fellows you played with, but these boys went out of their way to make it easy for me. Even from the beginning we were like one big happy family."

The "family" was the answer to a hockey coach's—or to a long suffering Bruin or Ranger fan's—dream. First, of course, there was Maurice Richard, a combination of Babe Ruth and Ty Cobb in one combustible package, a self-made, super-mad athlete of ferocious intensity, who always played hockey as if he were waging a one-man war. At the Verdun training camp the Rocket, getting set to embark upon his 13th National Hockey League season, impressed observers as being more relaxed than he had ever been before. But still all the Montreal hands crossed their fingers; one never knew about Richard.

The second superstar in camp was Jean Beliveau, who the previous season had just begun to live up to his ballyhoo. Beliveau was—and is—a strikingly handsome man of big proportions: six feet, three inches tall, 210 pounds. A wonderful stickhandler, a picture skater, a perfect team man with a sense of play-making that approaches pure aesthetics, Beliveau is like a DiMaggio on the ice: cool, classic, noncha-lantly graceful. His play always seems so effortless that it is hard to realize how much intelligence and skill go into it. As one Montrealer puts it: "Unless you've ever played hockey yourself, it's impossible to realize how many difficult things Beliveau can do, do well, and yet make it look so easy." The fourth highest all-time goal scorer in hockey, Beliveau is as sophisticated and self-assured a personality as one meets on the sports beat. But at that time he was still awkwardly shy for he was just beginning to find himself, to step out of the shell that he had enclosed himself in during his first two years as a Canadien.

JEAN BELIVEAU

If Beliveau was emerging, if the Rocket was seasoning, the most tension-packed player at Verdun was Bernie

"Boom Boom" Geoffrion. A two-time winner of the Art Ross Trophy, the fifth highest goal scorer of all time (371) Geoffrion was rated by such knowledgeable hockey men as Lynn Patrick as the greatest scorer of them all. But winning the scoring trophy for the first time had caused Geoffrion more heartache than glory. For when he swept ahead of the idled idol, Richard, at the end of the 1954-55 season to win the scoring championship by a single point, the Forum fans refused to forgive him. They booed him at the arena, they jeered him in the street, they even threatened his life over the phone. "What could I do?" he recalls. "It was not my fault the Rocket was suspended. The team was still fighting for first. I couldn't deliberately not score. So I was sick of the whole thing. Even thinking about hockey made me throw up. I wanted to get away from hockey. But then before practices began Beliveau and Richard visited me. And they urged me to stay in the game."

Not as stylish as Beliveau, not as instinctive as Richard Geoffrion was nevertheless a strong skater, a powerful checker, a fine stickhandler—and there was his shot; his blazing slapshot. "It made our power play," says Blake. Drawing his stick back in an arc about two feet from the puck, and then swinging at it like a golfer making an approach shot, Geoffrion effected a shot that was extremely accurate, swift and difficult to stop.

Boom Boom had enough color in his own right to light up a town, but unfortunately for his brooding character the town was not Montreal, not during this period in which he was forced to stand in the shadow of the Rocket's glare. Gifted with both a vivid imagination and dramatic extremes of mood, he could shake up a dressing room when he was "high" or vanish into the woodwork when he was "low." But on the ice he was always as dedicated a player as one could wish for.

Like Geoffrion, Dickie Moore was then a player who was just beginning to realize his full potential. A pleasant enough young man off the ice, he seemed to skate as if a chip had been implanted upon his shoulders. At this point his most notable talent was his ability to "swing," to play either wing and to fit in with any line. He could shoot hard, pass unerringly and perform extremely cleverly with the puck; he was the thinking man's hockey player. Many NHL veterans still consider Moore—the holder of the NHL record for the most points in one season: 96—one of the most underrated players of his time.

Left wing Bert Olmstead was also underrated. "Of the boys on that team I don't know if they ever gave Olmstead all his dues," says Blake. A scuffler and a digger, Olmstead excelled at positional play. On offense he would get rid of the puck quickly, laying down firm passes; his defensive ability could only be compared to that of Ted Lindsay. Always teamed with offensive thinking stars, he had to be a brutal and tenacious checker. There was also an arrogance to his composure— a sneer, or at least a smirk, always seemed to play upon his lips—that did not serve to endear him to rivals. It was an expression of his confident belief in victory. "I don't care what they call me," he would say, "I don't care how much they hate me—as long as we win."

Rounding out the first two lines in training camp was veteran Kenny Mosdell. Long and lean of build—as was Olmstead—he had just placed on the league's All-Star team for two years in a row. Quiet and unassuming, his stardom as a scorer had come late—in each of those past two seasons he had contributed 22 goals; before he had been better known as a checker and a penalty killer.

"Your style of coaching has to depend upon the players you have," says Blake. "because if you try to change the styles of your players you're in trouble. If you're connected with so many superstars as I was, then you've got to let them go all out and let the defense look after itself. And, fortunately, I had a defense that could look after itself. I had my superstars there, too. Doug Harvey was the greatest defenseman who ever played hockey—bar none; and over a five-year period beginning that season Jacques Plante was the greatest goalie the League has ever seen."

DOUG HARVEY

Doug Harvey, a six-time winner of the Norris Trophy awarded to the League's outstanding backliner, was the complete defenseman. "Usually a defenseman specializes in one thing and builds a reputation on that," says Blake, "but Doug could do everything well. He was less colorful than an Eddie Shore so he never got the recognition he deserved," says Blake. But Harvey lacked color the way a blue-chip stock lacks glamour. He was probably the only player in hockey to be as "cool" as the surface the game is played upon. Often Harvey's cool was mistaken for disinterest. Actually, it was the result of an always calculating concentration. Besides being able to break up an enemy rush, to backcheck with effortless finesse, Harvey could inaugurate a play from farther back and carry it farther forward than any other defenseman. Quick to capitalize on any lapse, the cogs would be turning over in his brain and an attack would be programmed by the time he reached the blue line. However, if the right man failed to get free for the right pass, Harvey would remain unflustered, maneuvering with the puck until an optional attack could mount.

If aloof in his playing style, he was consistent also in his attitude toward both opponents and fans. He refused to shake the hands of any rival in the gesture of sportsmanship; he would never patronize the fans in any way. The quarterback of the team on the ice, he was also the leader of the team off the ice. He was the spokesman, the social hub, the center about whom the company always formed.

Goalies are usually the "loners" on a club—they seldom have teammates to compare notes with—and Plante was no exception. He also suffered asthmatic attacks which made it impossible for him to stay with the rest of the team at certain hotels. But Plante, a six-time winner of the Vezina Trophy, was very much at home in the nets—or, at least, in using them as a base from which to go wandering. For Plante singlehandedly revolutionized the concept of goaltending in hockey. Operating on the principle that possession was nine-tenths of the ice law, Plante would stray from the protective crease, leaving his net as exposed as the model in a *Playboy* centerfold, to track down pucks, retrieve them, and whisk them back to the proper Canadien channels. He could afford to be adventurous because he was an unusually fast skater. And his speed wasn't confined solely to his feet. His vision, his hands, his reaction time were all uncommonly swift; his reflexes were cobra-quick. In the net he was given to making remarkable saves; the only contemporary in his class was Terry Sawchuck.

Not only a "walking" goalie, Plante was also a talking goalie. A keen and alert student of the game, an intellectual on ice, he would constantly issue forth a stream of instructions from his embattled vantage point: "Get it, Harvey . . . Move over, Johnson . . . Look out for Howe . . . Go, Rocket, Go!" Inventive and resourceful, later in his career he came up with an otherworldly goalie mask. But in the autumn of 1955, his bare face— lean, high cheek bones, hollowed eyes—could still be seen scrupulously regarding the approach of a puck.

"It took everybody a long time to know that Tom Johnson was as good as we knew he was," Blake says of Harvey's defensive tandem mate. Just as Geoffrion played Hubert Humphrey to Richard's Lyndon Johnson, so too was Tom Johnson obscured by his superstar partner. Six feet tall, a sturdy 180 pounds, Johnson concentrated on the aggressive duties of a defenseman. A furious checker and an inveterate brawler, he was, in the opinion of Frank Selke, a better "defensive" defenseman than Harvey.

Out of uniform Johnson was a gay blade, a charmer, a free spender. A bachelor, he read voraciously, had gourmet tastes, and dated beautiful and intelligent women. The five or six parties he would throw each year for the team were the social highlights of the season.

Rounding out his defensemen Blake had the tough veteran Butch Bouchard, the team captain, who was starting his 15th season as a Canadien; Bob Turner, a skilled penalty killer; Dolly St. Laurent, a handy "spot" blueliner; and Jean Guy Talbot, a promising rookie. And up front for his third line he planned to go with another rookie, Claude Provost; a fiery sophomore, Jackie LeClair; and Floyd "Busher" Curry, a player who was always capable of rising to an occasion: he scored the only hat trick of his career on the night Queen Elizabeth visited The Forum. Along with rookie Don Marshall, the remaining forward on the roster, Curry would turn in a most creditable job at the stick-check, ice-the-puck, team-bottling duties of penalty killing in the season to come.

One more forward was in camp. He wasn't even listed on the roster; he was still eligible for another year in "junior" competition; and yet he presented the greatest threat to the calm atmosphere of determination that Selke and Blake were trying to set. Not that this small five-feet, seven-inch 155 pounder was ever heard to utter a single offensive word—in either French or English—to anyone. In fact, he hardly spoke at all. It was just that this 19-year-old stripling happened to be the Rocket's kid brother, Henri.

"Every time I looked up at practice," Blake recalls, "the Pocket had the puck. I couldn't think of leaving him off the squad. But I still didn't know what to do about him. We figured we'd never be able to put the two Richards together: they'd always be looking for each other; or if the Pocket got into a scrape, someone picked on him, the Rocket would be over in a second and explode. We didn't want that to happen. So for awhile I really didn't know what to do, where I would play him."

One afternoon Blake was afraid his dilemma was resolved, but it was a frightening solution that presented itself. The two brothers, rounding the nets after a play, collided so violently that both were knocked cold. Blake held his breath until they came to. The Pocket required six stitches, the Rocket took 12 stitches. Finally, the Rocket spoke: "You better watch yourself, Henri. You might get hurt." But the Pocket, the fastest skater on the team, a man who would play 60 minutes if allowed, soon proved that it would be the rest of the league who would be hurting as he began to develop into a superstar in his own right.

The Canadiens inaugurated the season auspiciously with a shutout win over the Maple Leafs. Geoffrion was injured in that game but the Pocket filled in for him at right wing.

When Geoffrion returned to the lineup Blake was forced to reconsider the problem of the two Richards. "The team was going great. We had good harmony and good spirit and it was easy to maintain because we were winning," Blake recalls. "And Maurice wasn't exploding. Sometimes I had to cool him off right on the bench. He glared at me, but he took it from me. And so one game when we were losing by a few goals I decided I had to give it a try someday. So I put Henri in—instead of Mosdell—with the Rocket and Dickie Moore. And that became my second line. It didn't take the Rocket long to see that Henri was one guy he didn't have to protect."

Once the Rocket almost did blast off, though. At Madison Square Garden in the closing seconds of a period, Ranger bad boy Lou Fontinato cut open the

Rocket's eye with a punch. In the dressing room the Rocket burned with silent rage. Ken Reardon, former defenseman, who was a Canadien front office employee, came to the dressing room and did some eloquent fast talking. He pointed out that to everybody it had been obvious that Fontinato's punch had been a lucky one and that for the sake of the team it just wasn't worth risking another suspension over; he ought to do nothing about it. After Reardon's speech Doug Harvey cracked a tension-snapping joke. The team laughed, the Rocket smiled and a crisis was averted.

The Canadiens, as a team that season, often enjoyed themselves. Harvey had a quick and ready wit, Johnson always communicated a sense of joy, Dickie Moore had a keen appreciation of jokes and pranks, Geoffrion could get everybody laughing in two languages, and even the Rocket had a droll sense of humor. Once, Montreal *Weekend*'s sports editor, Andy O'Brien, was working on a photo-story of a Montreal to New York road trip. At the station all the players dutifully kissed their wives goodbye for the photographer—except the Rocket who continued to puff away solemnly on his cigar. O'Brien asked the Rocket if perhaps he didn't approve of kissing wives goodbye. "Not on the short trips," replied the Rocket.

Like most Canadien teams, the '55-56 team was not one to cause a coach headaches because of wild after-houring. Yet on one occasion, distraught over a loss, Blake tried to lay down a curfew. "I want everybody in bed at 11 o'clock," he told the team. "Gee, Coach," Harvey shot back, "does that mean we have to wait until 11 to go to bed?"

Blake since that season—with six Stanley Cups and seven Prince of Wales Trophies to his credit—has generally come to be recognized as one of the greatest hockey men of our time. "Sure, Blake had a bunch of stars," says Frank Selke, recalling the '55-56 season, "but he moulded them into a team. I think something of Blake as a player rubs off on any of his teams. He was a star but not a superstar. What he achieved came from sheer guts and go. He is impatient only with those who won't work, and is comfortable as an old shoe to have around."

Just as Blake was developing his qualities as a leader, the team was showing its league mastery. The outcome of the race was decided conclusively on the nights of January 29, February 2 and February 4. For on those three nights, with but 20 games left to play, the Canadiens met with their arch enemies, the Red Wings, the winners of the NHL championship seven years in a row.

Montreal entered the series with a 10-point margin over the second place Wings. The first game, in Detroit, ended in a 1-1 tie. The second game, also in Detroit, went to the Canadiens, 2-0, when Montreal scored two goals in two minutes late in the first period. First, the Rocket took a pass from the Pocket and slapped a low sizzler past goalie Glenn Hall. Then, Beliveau scored by rifling a Bert Olmstead pass through Hall's legs. For Plante it was the seventh shutout of the season.

In the third game, in Montreal, the Wings took an early lead. With Rocket Richard in the penalty box, Ted Lindsay scored for Detroit. But the Canadiens tied the game when Beliveau dribbled in a goal with Hall out of position. And then in the beginning of the third period, Olmstead pulled a classic play, the carom play. He jabbed the puck against the boards, wheeled around Wing defenseman Godfrey, and relayed the puck to Beliveau, who picked it up on the end of his stick and scored the winning goal.

Montreal emerged from the series with a 15-point spread. The battle for first place was over and Montrealers impatiently waited for March 20—the day the Stanley Cup playoffs started.

In the semi-finals, the Canadiens faced off against the New York Rangers. It was easy. The Canadiens won the first game, 7-1, with the Rocket scoring three goals, Boom Boom two, and Dickie Moore and Beliveau one apiece. Montreal lost the second game, won the third and fourth and beat the Rangers in the fifth, 7-0. The surprise in the fifth game came not from the fact that the Pocket, Doug Harvey and Dickie Moore each scored a pair of goals while Beliveau scored one, but in the passing of the Rocket; he was credited with five assists. After the game he happily announced: "Now I have become a playmaker."

In the other semi-finals series, the Red Wings turned back Toronto in five games. Now, the showdown—another dramatic Montreal-Detroit Cup finale. Some Forum fans pitched tents in front of the general admission windows for the few general admission seats that would go on sale the day of the opening game.

The turning point in the Detroit-Montreal series came in the first game. And it came because of the play of the Canadiens' unsung, unheralded third or "checking" line of LeClair, Provost and Curry. "In play-offs, your big stars are checked pretty closely," says Blake. "And if your third line can sneak in for a goal or two, you can win it; when they don't, you lose it."

With five minutes gone in the third period Detroit led, 4-2. It was then that the third line "sneaked" in.

LeClair and Curry got the puck out in a scramble behind the Red Wing net. LeClair swooped in with it and scored. Then, within 60 seconds, Guy Talbot made a beautiful run the length of the rink and passed the puck to Geoffrion, who whizzed a shot home, tying the score at 4-4.

Seventy-one seconds later, Boom Boom shot again, Beliveau took the rebound and scored with it. Three minutes later, LeClair grabbed off the puck in heavy milling and passed it to Provost who punched it in for the goal. In slightly more than five minutes the Canadiens had exploded for four goals, two of them coming from their third line. Detroit not only lost, 6-4, but they lost in the most demoralizing way: with Montreal coming from behind and led by reserves.

The second game went to Montreal 5-1; again a "little gun" triggered the scoring. Don Marshall scored the first goal from 15 feet out at 7:22 of the first period before the big guns—The Pocket, the Rocket, the Boom, and Le Gros Bill Beliveau—each found the range.

The series moved to Detroit for the third game and the Red Wings won, 3-1. It looked like a traditional Detroit-Montreal "homer" finals might develop.

The Red Wings, led by Red Kelly, began the fourth game, in Detroit, by playing primarily a defensive game, bottling up the Canadien attack as they waited for a break. But the break never came. Late in the first period Beliveau stormed in to knock a Olmstead rebound into the net. The Red Wings then changed their tactics, turning to the attack themselves. Plante, however, made one impossible save after another, and the Red Wings never scored. Montreal scored twice more, another by Beliveau and one by Curry—again that third line—for a

3-0 shutout. Not only Detroit's "service," but the Red Wing heart was all but broken.

The series returned to Montreal with the Canadiens leading 3-1 and excitement gripping Montreal. A wild crowd of 14,151 kill-happy fans filled the Forum, hoping to see Detroit beaten down once and for all.

The first period was scoreless, Glenn Hall and Plante coming up with clutch saves. Excitement mounted as more than two-thirds of the second period elapsed without a score. Suddenly there was a breakthrough.

The crucial blow was set up by Doug Harvey. Playing with the puck, forcing Detroit to commit itself, Harvey waited until Floyd "Busher" Curry got loose from Gordie Howe, then shot him a lead pass. Curry, in turn, swept the puck over to the racing Beliveau who masterfully beat Hall with a whirling backhander. It was Jean's 12th goal of the playoffs.

Fifty-two seconds later the Rocket scored. In the third period, Boom Boom scored.

Detroit scored once on a Delvecchio goal. And that was all. Then came the riot . . .

The Forum fans rioted with joy. The Fat Cup was pushed out onto the ice and captain Butch Bouchard accepted it on behalf of the team and then they all drank champagne from it. The team continued its celebration in the dressing room and the jubilant fans swept out onto Ste. Catherine Street and flowed like a New Year's Eve crowd down toward the center of town. The players and their wives taxied over to Bouchard's "Chez Butch" in the East End and partied there until dawn.

The next day—while the Red Wings quietly slipped out of town—Montreal honored its dream team with a 30-mile parade. Perhaps to some Montrealers it was as if

Bonnie Prince Charlie had become king, perhaps to others it was like the restoration of a Bourbon dynasty. But all of hockey-mad Montreal was happy—in any language.

For Beliveau it was the incomparable thrill of his first Stanley Cup. For Geoffrion it meant finding acceptance again in his hockey home. For the Rocket Richard it was the honoring of a promise, the fulfillment of a prophecy. For the rookie coach Toe Blake it meant security in his new job. And for the zealous partisans of the Canadiens it was the beginning of what Camil DesRoches, the former Montreal publicist, wistfully calls "those five wonderful years."

Rocky Marciano's Musketeer

On September 21, 1955, Rocky Marciano knocked out Archie Moore in what would be the final fight of his career, allowing him to retire as heavyweight champion with a spotless 49-0 record. By any standard, Marciano was an unlikely champion. At 5-foot-10, 185 pounds, he was a small heavyweight. His reach was the shortest of any heavyweight champion in boxing history, and his boxing style was crude, better suited for ballroom brawling than prize fighting, or so it seemed. But he was fearless and relentless. In the following article, written a year after Marciano's final fight, Frank Graham, Jr. provides a fascinating look at the champion as seen through the eyes of Marciano's life-long friend, Allie Colombo. As boys, they were next-door neighbors, and as adults they remained side by side through Marciano's 49 fights despite attempts by Marciano's trainer, Al Weill, to tear them apart.

By Frank Graham, Jr.

December 1956

THIS WAS IN 1952 and Rocky Marciano, the newly-crowned heavyweight champion of the world, was touring a remote area of his domain, the islands of the western Pacific. With him were his manager, Al Weill, his trainer, Charley Goldman, and a couple of sparring partners. In the Philippines, the wandering band paid a visit to an island where a colony of lepers, cut off from the rest of humanity, lived out their unhappy days. The champion, an object of awe and admiration wherever his travels took him, put on a boxing exhibition for the lepers and told them he would answer any questions about himself or boxing that might occur to them. There was a moment of silence, and then one of the sufferers raised his hand.

"What's your question?" Rocky asked him.

"Tell me," the man said, looking over the Marciano entourage, "where is Allie Colombo?"

Allisay Colombo, who was born on Brook Street in Brockton, Mass., and grew up next door to a sturdy youngster named Rocco Marchegiano, hitched his wagon to a star and now he has his own home and money in the bank and his name is known in strange corners of the earth. Allie didn't win the championship, but his pal did, and that was the next best thing. Before Marciano, the great heavyweight champions had sprung, full-grown, from some glamorous obscurity: Jack Johnson had fought his way up from the docks and the lusty honky-tonks of Galveston, Jack Dempsey had come roaring out of the hobo jungles of the Far West and Joe Louis had appeared, like a dark avenger, out of nowhere. But Rocky Marciano was the kid next door, and Allie was at his side every step of the way.

"Even as kids, we had a championship complex in our neighborhood," Allie will tell you as he lounges in a canvas chair on his big lawn. From that lawn he can look across Harlan Circle to the lawn and the attractive house of the retired undefeated heavyweight champion. "All the teams we played on, baseball, softball, football or basketball, won titles. We thought like champions."

They were Brockton champions, of course, not world champs. But Rocky, who was four years younger than Colombo, could lick anybody in the neighborhood and anybody on the teams they played, too, and whenever a brawl started, his teammates were sure that he gave them an edge. There was a fierce loyalty among the kids who made Edgar Playground their base, and playing games was the only thing in the world they cared about. If Rocky could lick the toughest guys in Brockton, then they reasoned he could lick the toughest guys in any other town. So Allie and Rocky talked it over and they set out to win the heavyweight championship of the world. It was preposterous and maybe even harebrained, but that is what they set out to do.

The fierce loyalty which Marciano had picked up around the playground in Brockton has been a part of him ever since and so it was natural that his lifetime pal, Allie Colombo, would become a permanent member of his troupe once the impossible had happened. Of course, to get what you want in the curious and savage world of boxing, you have to have a crafty manager, and Rocky put himself under the influence of one of the craftiest, Al Weill. When you're in the ring with the tough fighters you meet on the way to the top, and your face is cut and your eyes are blinded by punches, you must have an experienced handler in your corner, and Charley Goldman, one of the most experienced, became Rocky's trainer. And in the background were the inevitable sinister figures who hang around the fight game and move in like wolves at the sight of a powerful young man who can punch the way Rocky Marciano could. Yet such was Rocky's loyalty that Colombo went all the way with him and got his just share of every purse.

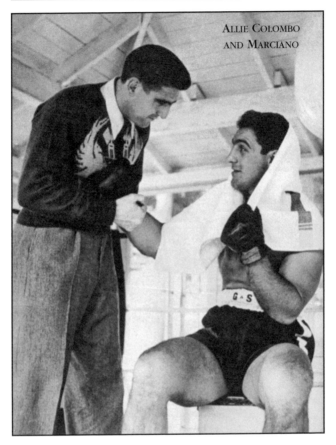

ALLIE COLOMBO
AND MARCIANO

Allie had some unofficial titles in the days when Marciano held the championship; he was called Rocky's co-manager and his assistant trainer. But mostly he was Rocky's pal. He would go on the road with Rocky in the mornings when the champion was in training, and they would while away the long evenings talking out some of their problems and planning for the future. And as the days went by and the training became drudgery, Allie would prop up Rocky's spirits by telling jokes and by imitating the malevolent Weill, a routine which Rocky found particularly diverting.

"I wish everybody found me as funny as Rocky does," Colombo says. "Then I could get my own television show."

Allie, who began seconding Marciano in the ring when he was an amateur, was still a regular in his corner, along with Weill and Goldman, when Rocky was the champion of the world. Each man had his own duties; Weill, almost apoplectic under the tension, would scream his instructions to Rocky, Goldman would handle cuts, bruises or whatever other emergencies might arise during the course of a fight, and Allie would swab Rocky's tongue with a cold sponge.

"Rocky, never gargled during a fight," Allie says. "When he was boxing in the amateurs one night, somebody, not me, rammed a bottle of water into his mouth and in the excitement just kept pushing on it. Rocky almost choked to death. After that whenever anybody tried to give him a drink between rounds, he would always pull away. So I'd have the sponge ready when he came back to the corner and he'd stick his tongue and I'd wipe it for him."

Even when Rocky was strangling, there couldn't have been as many hectic moments in his corner during his amateur and early professional fights as there were after Weill decided that his young heavyweight had advanced to a point where Alphonse could resign his post as matchmaker at Madison Square Garden and take an active part in seconding him between rounds. Weill, whose complete and stifling domination of Rocky eventually led to the champion's retirement, had to be the master every moment he was around.

"I knew Weill was a good manager," Allie says, "and so I thought he would be a very efficient guy in a corner, too. I couldn't believe a guy could get as excited as he did during a fight. It was a panic in our corner. Weill couldn't look up because he said it made him dizzy, so while the fight was going on he'd hear the crowd roar and he'd shout to me. 'What's going on now?' I'd tell him, and then right away he'd say again, 'What happened? Did Rocky get hit?' And I'd tell him. I'd spend the whole fight giving him a blow-by-blow description.

"Then Weill would say, 'What should Rocky be doing?' And Goldman or I would tell him he should be using his left more or punching to the body, and Weill would say, 'All right, all right, don't you tell him! I'll tell him.' And when the round would be over we'd all jump in the ring and Weill would yell, 'Don't say anything! I'll do the talking!' And he'd start to holler at Rocky. It was a lucky thing Rocky's such a calm guy. He'd just sit there and never say a word."

While there is no doubt that Colombo often resented the lordly and upsetting presence of the tubby manager at ringside and around the training camps, he is quick to admit that Weill was the genius who smoothed Rocky's path to the championship. The resentment stemmed from Weill's attitude toward Allie, whom he considered a nuisance and the only barrier to his complete domination of the fighter. Allie, for a time, was also genuinely concerned that Weill's frantic and unnerving antics between rounds would upset Rocky and cause him to do less than his best.

In his 12th professional bout, Marciano met Gilley

Ferron in Philadelphia. It was the first time Weill had worked in his corner and Rocky, wanting to make a good impression on his manager, especially because of the alarming state of excitement into which Al had worked himself, was over-eager. He threw punches like a small boy heaving rocks and, though he knocked out Ferron in the second round, he came out of the fight with a broken hand. Colombo placed the blame on Weill and was relieved when Al shortly afterward became matchmaker at the Garden and was prohibited from working in his fighter's corner. When Weill later resigned that post Allie told Marciano of his fears and Rocky said he would discreetly suggest to Weill that he stick to managing and let Goldman and Colombo minister to him in the ring.

Weill was desolate. "Rocky," he said, his voice tinged with shocked surprise, "you know whatever I do is for your own good. Where did you ever get an idea like that?"

Rocky dropped the matter and did not bring it up again. Weill continued to work in his corner and Colombo, accepting the situation as best he could, gained a measure of satisfaction by mimicking the manager behind his back, always to Rocky's grinning delight.

The Marciano-Colombo partnership dates back to childhood. The two families grew up next door to each other and each produced its share of athletes. Lou Colombo, Allie's cousin, was considered a fine prospect for a time in the Brooklyn Dodgers' minor-league organization, while Rocky's brother, Lou, played class D ball in Florida last summer. When Allie was about 13, his uncle brought home a portable boxing ring and set it up in his back yard. Allie made his first venture into boxing then, promoting a bout between the nine-year-old Rocky and another husky neighborhood boy who was a couple of years older. Rocky, of course, won.

When Allie got a paper route, he talked Rocky into helping him make the door-to-door deliveries. Naturally, the junior member of the partnership wound up doing most of the work. This business enterprise came to an abrupt end when a circulation man from the newspaper came upon Allie sitting on the curb reading the sports pages while little Rocco trudged up the block with a man-sized load of papers under his arm. But this juvenile exploitation never discouraged Rocky and, before he was old enough to play baseball and football with the older boys, he was their loudest rooter during the games at Edgar Playground. When Allie became a playing manager, he always made sure that Rocky had a chance to play, and the future champion soon became one of the better sandlot athletes in the city of Brockton. In 1941, Colombo joined the Army and the friendship that had sprung up between these two sports-crazy boys came temporarily to an end.

Allie served with the Air Transport Command during the war and was stationed first in Detroit and then in India. He lost track of Rocky until he returned to the States and was serving in the transportation office at Westover Field in Massachusetts. Somebody had told him that Rocky was at Fort Lewis in Washington, and one evening, when a soldier passed through his office on the way back to Fort Lewis from an emergency furlough, Colombo asked him if he had ever heard of his pal, Rocky Marchegiano.

"Oh, you mean the fighter," the soldier said.

Allie was only mildly surprised by the soldier's description of Rocky. Though his friend had never even had an amateur fight around Brockton, it was natural to think of Rocky, the rugged kid who had been so formidable in those playground brawls, as a fighter. The soldier reached into his bag and pulled out a camp newspaper and there, in a front-page photo, his arms raised in the classic boxing pose and his mouth set in a grim line, was Rocky Marchegiano. Questioning the soldier, Allie learned that Rocky was boxing in camp shows and was knocking some pretty good fighters dead with his smashing right hand.

Finally the war was over and Allie and Rocky both came back to Brockton. There was no such stir as was touched off by their later returns to the city, and they settled into the pleasantly aimless life of athletic bums. They played semi-pro baseball and football and hung around the Ward 2 Club and passed the time talking about Ted Williams and Lou Boudreau and Joe Louis and Jersey Joe Walcott. When things really got tough, they went out and got jobs, usually as laborers, but none of the jobs lasted long and pretty soon they were back at more congenial pursuits.

It was about this time that Rocky began boxing as an amateur, with Allie acting as his manager and chief second. Rocky inflicted as much damage on himself as he did on his opponents. Each time his fist landed against another man's jawbone, there was considerable doubt which bony object would shatter first, the fist or the jaw. Rocky was plagued by broken hands until Charley Goldman taught him how to hold them in 1949.

Meanwhile, through a former fighter named Dick O'Connor, whom he had met in the Army, Allie got his pal a four-round professional bout in Holyoke on February 21, 1947. Allie understood that Rocky was to get $50 for the fight. They paid $15 for a license and $5 for a professional second. After the fight, which Rocky won by a knockout in the third round, the promoter said he had made no agreement to give them $50, and that all he could pay was $35.

"I put up an awful holler," Allie says, "and finally the promoter came back with two cops and said, 'Throw these guys out of here.' Rocky was standing there and he was getting madder every minute, not as mad as I was, but pretty mad, and finally he said to me, 'Let me belt this guy.' The two cops moved in to calm him down, and while everybody was arguing I went into the office and told the guy who was counting the money that the promoter said it was okay to give me the extra 15 bucks. Believe it or not, he forked it over, and I rushed out and grabbed Rocky, who was still hollering at the promoter, and pulled him out of there.

"Outside we met O'Connor, the guy who had arranged the fight, and he took us around to some political club he belonged to. A political club! It looked like some crummy dungeon, with a bar on one side of the room. O'Connor said that when John L. Sullivan won a fight, he'd go into a joint and buy everybody there a drink and that's what Rocky should do. So we walked in and there were a few guys sitting around drinking beer and playing cards. Rocky was kind of embarrassed but he spoke up and said, 'I'm buying for the house.' Everybody looked up, surprised for a second, then they dropped their cards and their beer and rushed up to the bar to order Scotch. Rocky paid for the drinks and then I hustled him out of there before it cost us any more dough."

Rocky had made a reputation for himself as a catcher around Brockton, and when he got a chance for a tryout with a farm team of the Chicago Cubs in 1948, Allie and Rocky talked it over. "Go ahead," Allie told him. "You've always wanted to be a ballplayer. If it doesn't work out, you've still got time to be a fighter." Rocky went to Fayettesville, N.C., survived the first cut but lost out on the second and the die was cast. He was doomed to be a fighter.

Rocky had used the name of Rocky Mack in his one professional fight, so he was still able to enter amateur tournaments under his own name. Several impressive performances in the Golden Gloves and other amateur tournaments convinced Allie that, with the proper training, his pal could lick anybody who might be foolish enough to climb in a ring with him, and he talked Rocky into believing it, too. Rocky, whose confidence in his ability to take care of himself was always considerable, didn't need much prompting. Here was the point where Allie performed perhaps his greatest service to Rocky's eventual success. Realizing that neither of them had the slightest inkling of how to get started in the intricate business of boxing, and remembering their experience in Holyoke, Allie logically reasoned that if Rocky was to become the best prizefighter in the world, he should have the best manager in the world. After several false starts, he finally came up with the right man. One day, he read a column about Al Weill written by Jack Cuddy, the United Press boxing writer, in which Cuddy pointed out some of Weill's virtues (boxing virtues, that is) and mentioned that he had piloted a couple of Italian boys, Lou Ambers and Marty Servo, to world championships. Allie sat down and wrote Weill a letter, asking for a tryout, and then went back to running his ball club.

They were at Edgar Playground when the call came

from Weill. Rocky, who was recovering from one of his numberless broken hands, was playing first base and Allie had put himself behind the bat. In the middle of the game, Allie's sister came running out on the field. "Allie, Allie," she called breathlessly. "You've got a long-distance call from Washington."

Allie knew what it was. Without bothering to take off his equipment, he rushed home, clumping down Brook Street in his shinguards, mask and chest protector. Weill, in Washington with one of his fighters, wanted him to bring Rocky to New York for a tryout.

Rocky's uncle, Mike Piccento, drove them to New York and the tryout was held in the CYO Gym. Charley Goldman, the little trainer who has handled a number of Weill's fighters, was there and he needed a lot of impressing. Rocky was not only absurdly awkward but, at 23, was pretty old to be just starting out. Goldman was also grumpy because Rocky owned no equipment and Charley had to find him a mouthpiece and headguard.

"Anyway" Allie says, "Rocky made a good impression. Weill was being cautious because he didn't want to go for any dough and he said he'd let us know. Sure enough, after a while we got a letter telling us he would manage Rocky."

There were still some lean days ahead. Weill was not going to invest any money in such a long-shot as this overage, awkward novice, and Rocky and Allie had to pay their own way. They went back to Brockton and got on the city payroll as highway laborers at $60 a week and then hitched rides to New York with friendly truck drivers once a week so that Rocky could have his injured hand treated by a doctor there. That winter, they boxed in the snow in Allie's back yard, protected from the cold by hooded jackets, Rocky punched only with his left hand.

When they moved to New York, they lived first with Goldman, on 92nd Street, but later moved to the Sloane House YMCA on 34th Street. In the mornings, they would walk up to Central Park and do their road-work, Allie keeping up doggedly with the inexhaustible Rocky and thereby becoming the best-conditioned manager who ever followed his fighter into a ring. In the afternoons, Rocky received boxing lessons from the patient Goldman.

"We didn't see much of Weill," Allie says. "In the evenings we ate in greasy spoon joints. I always had to laugh after Rocky got to be the champ and Weill was so particular about what Rocky had to eat. When we were broke, we ate in crummy little Spanish places because that kind of food was cheaper. Some of that hot stuff would have poisoned a horse.

"Then after dinner we used to walk up Broadway. It didn't take much to please us. Once in a while we'd see a celebrity like Jack Oakie. One night we saw Willie Pep with a girl and we followed them up the street. They were arguing because the girl wanted to go in one of the big movies on Broadway and Willie wanted to see something at one of the cheaper places on 42nd Street. Willie won the argument, and we were excited because we'd seen the featherweight champion of the world. Other nights we used to go over to a theater where a musical called *Too Many Girls* was playing and we'd just stand outside the stage door and watch the showgirls go in. They got used to seeing us there and once in a while one of them would say hello. I'd say hello back and Rocky thought I had a lot of guts to do that. Then, when we'd checked all the girls in, we'd turn around and head back for the 'Y'."

The two lonely young men made almost no friends in New York. They lived within themselves, walking unnoticed the crowded streets on which Rocky would hear himself acclaimed a few years afterward. They analyzed everything—the moves Rocky had made in the gym, the advice given them by Goldman, and their daily training routine. Finally the day came when Goldman decided Rocky was ready for his second professional "debut" and Weill arranged for Manny Almeida, who promoted fights in Providence, R.I., to handle the young heavyweight in his early bouts.

"You hit Joe Louis with that punch and you'll knock him out!" Those were the words with which Almeida greeted Marciano in the dressing room after Rocky had scored a one-round knockout in his first fight in Providence. One quick knockout followed another during 1948 as Almeida scoured New England for victims. Set-ups and tough guys, sluggers and cuties, they all fell before the devastating punches of this new heavyweight sensation.

"Rocky punched harder in those early fights than he ever did once he got to the top," Colombo will tell you. "Once he learned how to fight, he punched faster and in better combinations, but I know he lost some of that terrific power he had when he was flattening those guys in Providence. How he could belt!"

Meanwhile, Allie had already met the pretty blonde Lithuanian girl he would some day marry. Lilly was not only pretty, but her father had an old car that Allie and Rocky could use when they drove to Providence for a fight. It was a 1935 coupe and the brakes were terrible and the radiator was a miniature image of Yellowstone's

Old Faithful, but it was better than walking the 30 miles from Providence to Brockton, as they had done when they were a few years younger.

Now it was obvious to Weill that he had a tremendous prospect on his hands and he began to take a more active interest in him. The contract they had signed had stipulated that Rocky would get 60 per cent of each purse and Weill the other 40 per cent; Weill wouldn't agree to cut Colombo in for anything, although Allie had brought Rocky to him. From that time on, Rocky gave Allie ten per cent of each purse out of his own portion. Weill also had an agreement with another fight manager named Chick Wergeles, under which each manager gave the other a piece of whatever fighter they came across, so Wergeles got ten per cent of Weill's share. Frankie Carbo, a notorious underworld figure, has long been friendly with Weill and it was often rumored that he, too, was on the Marciano bandwagon, but to what extent, the New York State Athletic Commission and other interested parties could never determine.

Rocky and, of course, Allie were going only one way now—up—and there was but one bad moment along the way. On December 30, 1949, Marciano was matched with a young New York heavyweight named Carmine Vingo in a preliminary bout in Madison Square Garden. Vingo proved a tougher opponent than anybody realized he would be and Rocky, hurt in the early rounds, unleashed a terrific body attack that finally reduced Vingo to a stationary target. A couple of thunderous head punches completed his destruction. Vingo was rushed to a hospital with critical head injuries, and for days his life hung in the balance.

"We went over to St. Clare's Hospital and sat in the

lobby, just praying," Allie said. "I remember that the next night was New Year's Eve and we could hear the celebrating going on down the block, and it made us feel lousy. The worst part was when Vingo's family came in and Rocky didn't know whether he should even look at them. But a couple of them came over and told Rocky they held nothing against him, and that it was just an accident, and that made him feel better."

Vingo slowly recovered, and it is to Rocky's credit that he contributed money to his support until he was well enough to go to work. Carmine has since become a close friend of both Rocky and Allie.

Not long afterward, Rocky had his first main event in the Garden and won a split ten-round decision over Roland LaStarza. "I've often thought," Colombo says, "that the memory of the Vingo fight kept Rocky from opening up against LaStarza. It was the only fight Rocky ever had where there was any doubt about who won."

Two and a half years later, on September 23, 1952, Rocky stepped into the ring at Philadelphia's Municipal Stadium to fight Jersey Joe Walcott for the heavyweight championship of the world. He had destroyed all the other opposition in his path—Rex Layne, Joe Louis and Harry Mathews. He had won all of his 42 professional fights, 37 of them by knockouts. The city of Brockton had welcomed him home with a mammoth parade and celebration after his victory over Louis. There had even been a triumphal exhibition tour of the eastern states on which Rocky had been hailed as the coming champion.

"Chick Wergeles and I made that tour with Rocky," Allie says, laughing. "Wergeles has the guts of a burglar and whenever we came into a new town, we'd find out which was the best Italian restaurant there and we'd get him to call up the owner. Chick would say he was Rocky Marciano's manager and that he'd heard that the restaurant was going to invite Rocky and his pals there for a big Italian dinner. We ate free all over the East until we got to Maine. Those Yankees up there wouldn't fall for it.

"The tour was supposed to end in Boston on Christmas week, with Rocky putting on a boxing exhibition on the stage of the Old Howard burlesque theater. The Archbishop of Boston heard about it and put in a complaint, but Weill told him it was too late, that the contract had been signed. After the boxing exhibition, a sportswriter was supposed to interview Rocky on the stage, but the writer got sick and I took his place. Rocky and I had our dressing room right next to the top stripper in the show, and we passed the time listening to her practice her bumps and grinds."

Now the years of planning and working and hoping were over and Rocky was close to his goal. Allie had no doubts about his pal's ability to take the title from Walcott, but the tension leading up to the fight was terrific. For everybody except Rocky, that is. While he waited in the dressing room under the stands at Municipal Stadium, Rocky stretched out on a narrow bench in front of a row of lockers and went to sleep.

"There was nothing strange about it," Allie says. "It was getting on toward nine-thirty, which was his regular bedtime, anyway, so he naturally dozed off. I was supposed to wake him up so he could loosen up for a while before he went in the ring, but my watch stopped. I thought it was still only about nine-thirty when all of a sudden Weill came running into the dressing room. 'What's going on?' he yelled. 'He's supposed to be in the ring right now. Get him up!' We woke Rocky up and I grabbed a pail and the sponge and put an extra mouthpiece like I always did, in my back pocket, and off we went."

Weill, in his usual state of excitement, was bustling around, shouting orders and harassing Goldman and Colombo. At the end of the first round, in which Rocky had been on the floor, Weill was in a frenzy. When the buzzer sounded for the second round, he couldn't find Rocky's mouthpiece, but luckily Allie had brought the extra one. "Two days later, I was in a bar in Brockton," Allie says, "and a red-headed kid came up to me and said, 'Look what I got.' It was Rocky's mouthpiece. The kid said he had seen Weill take it out of Rocky's mouth and in the excitement throw it away. After the fight, the kid went over and picked it up as a souvenir.

"That was the first fight where I ever heard Rocky say anything between rounds. At the end of the sixth, he came back to the corner and said, 'I can't see.' We poured ice cold water into his eyes and it seemed to help some. He took some awful shots for a while, but when he came back after the 12th round, it was like he was coming out of a daze. 'How's it going?' he asked Weill, and Weill said, 'You got to knock him out.' He seemed to sit up straighter. He put his two gloves together under his chin, kind of bracing himself, and I said to Goldman, 'He's going to get this guy.'"

Rocky got his man in the next round and he was the new champion. One of the wildest scenes in boxing history followed as all of Brockton, or so it seemed, tried to climb into the ring and congratulate their hero. "I started up the steps even before the referee counted '10', but Weill grabbed my arm to pull himself up after me and tore the watch right off my wrist. The mob came piling over the newspapermen at the ringside and even the cops got into the ring just to jump around. The only guy they threw out was Rocky's old man, who was the only guy that really belonged, in there with him."

Allie, of course, belonged in there, too. It was his night to shout and jump around the ring and share with Rocky the crowning moment of their unlikely quest. That night there was a rousing party at a Philadelphia hotel, and later Allie and Lilly, who was now his wife, went to a night club. "What a night!" Allie said. "The master of ceremonies came out and announced there were two celebrities in the house. First he introduced Bobby Shantz, who was having that great year with the Athletics, and the crowd gave him a big hand. Then they introduced me as the manager of the new heavyweight champion, and I got an even bigger hand than the one they'd given Shantz."

Wedding bells were breaking up Rocky's old gang. Rocky himself had married in 1950, after getting permission from Weill to take the step, and Allie was married in 1952, shortly before the Walcott fight. As soon as he got back from his honeymoon, he headed for Marciano's training camp, leaving Lilly behind in Brockton.

"Lilly and I had talked it over," Allie says, "and she realized that for a few years I would be away from home a lot. Then, when we arranged that tour to the Pacific islands after Rocky won the title, I was all set to go, but Lilly put her foot down. 'I know you've got to go to Rocky's camp,' she said, 'but there's no reason why you have to go on those long tours with him.'" So in the interest of domestic harmony, Allie let other companions go with Rocky on the long tours.

There was one period when it seemed Rocky would

have to come up with another chief second, too. During the second fight with Ezzard Charles in New York, Marciano's corner was in its usual state of excitement. Weill, his head down, was shouting words of encouragement, advice and warning to his fighter, while Allie was keeping Weill advised of current developments. The deputy boxing commissioners posted in Marciano's corner thought Allie was doing the shouting, a practice which violates commission rules, and they kept warning him to keep quiet. The steady badgering from Weill on the one side and the deputies on the other was too much for Allie; finally, he turned on the commissioners and told them, in a strongly-worded message, what he thought of them.

"A few days after the fight," Allie recalls, "I read in the paper where my license had been revoked 'for conduct detrimental to boxing.' You'd have thought I fixed a fight or something. Finally Rocky went to the commission and squared the rap for me, but I was pretty upset for a while."

Two pretty little daughters, Cindy, four, and Jean, seven months, provide the bulk of Allie's excitement today. Although he has partially slipped back into the oblivion from which he and Rocky sprang seven years ago, there are moments when the old glory returns. When a national magazine paid Rocky $65,000 for the rights to his life story, the retired champion saw that Colombo was included in the deal. Allie got $7,500 to put into his six-room house on Harlan Circle.

"I'm still with Rocky," Allie says today. "We worked together on the life story, and we're hoping, of course, that it will be made into a movie. I think the money he got this year from the magazine story, plus whatever he gets next year from a movie or anything else like that, will give him enough to keep him from making a comeback. If he came back later, it would mean that he'd had a layoff of almost three years, and that's too long for a guy who depended on physical condition as much as Rocky did.

"Weill killed the goose that laid the golden egg. He dominated Rocky so much that he couldn't make a public appearance or even visit his family unless he got Weill's permission. Then Weill kept sending him on these long tours, and Rocky never had any time for himself. That's the big reason why he quit."

For some time, there have been reports that if Marciano decided to come out of retirement, he would ignore Weill and fight under Colombo's management alone. That is improbable because both Rocky and Allie are aware that most of Weill's faults stemmed from his intense desire to have a heavyweight champion, an attitude that could only help them. "You got to admire him," Allie says. "He wanted to win as bad as we did."

Allie would like to remain in boxing, and he has already tasted disappointment with several young fighters in whom he thought he saw possibilities. The hope is strong in him that some day he will come up with another sturdy kid with rocks in his fists and a body of armor plate who will blast his way to the championship. And why not? Allie Colombo caught lightning in a bottle once before.

What's In It For Sugar Ray Robinson?

In 1955, Sugar Ray Robinson came out of retirement to make some money but what he earned by reclaiming his middle-weight crown was a new measure of respect. Though widely regarded today as the best pound-for-pound fighter in history, in 1955, Robinson, 35, was a 4-1 underdog in his showdown against the champ, Carl "Bobo" Olson. The fight lasted less than two full rounds, ending when Robinson knocked out Olson to regain the title he had abandoned in 1952. The victory was as stunning as the story behind it was sad. It was a tale, as recounted by John Ross, of how a sports icon lost everything and was forced back into the ring to survive.

BY JOHN M. ROSS
MAY 1956

A CROWD GATHERED quickly as the gaudy, fuchsia-tinted Cadillac convertible eased up to the curb in New York's bustling Harlem. A hastily-rented string of flags decorated a row of store-fronts and from the canopy of a bar and grill dangled a hand-painted sign with the message:

Welcome home, Champ!
Your undying determination prevailed!

A mild roar went up from the gathering when Sugar Ray Robinson stepped from the car. Gawking motorists paused and honked their horns in salute, and Sugar Ray was all but swallowed up by the well-wishing herd. They struggled to pump his hand or pound his back. One robust woman, weeping profusely, threw her large arms around him and planted a crimson kiss on his forehead.

It was a moment Robinson had dreamed of many nights, a moment for which he struggled tortuously and prayed. He was caught in its emotional grip. Tears rolled freely down his bronze cheeks and he could barely mumble the usual courtesies to his admirers.

It was a familiar scene, one that had been staged many times during Ray's dramatic boxing career as he piled conquest upon conquest, glory upon glory. But, although it was familiar, it was strange, too. Only a few short weeks before, he had been pitied—even, in some cases, ridiculed—by these same people. They passed him by in the street without a nod. Only 48 hours earlier, when Ray had climbed through the ropes of Chicago Stadium to meet Carl (Bobo) Olson, few of them would have bet a lead nickel on his chances.

They had said Sugar Ray was finished, that his desperate comeback was bound to fail. It was not merely the consensus of opinion in Harlem. Shrewd boxing men everywhere agreed. So did the bookmakers. They made Olson a booming, 4-1 favorite, and there were few takers. That was the tip-off—no one had ever dared to stack the odds that high against Robinson.

It was a cruel appraisal. Indeed, it must have saddened the hearts of many who once marveled at the Sugar Ray of old. But it was accurate. Every rule in the book dictated it. Robinson was 35, an old man in a young man's game. In his stops along the comeback trail he had looked to be a pale carbon-copy of the great fighting machine that had won all but six of 143 fights. His reflexes were slow, his lightning-fast combinations gone. Second-raters who wouldn't have laid a glove on him in his heyday found him easy to clobber. He could go six fast rounds but after that his stamina seemed to desert him rapidly.

Once in the ring with Olson, however, it took Sugar Ray less than six minutes to rewrite the whole book—to destroy the legend that they never come back. Reaching back to yesterday like a fellow humming an old, familiar song, Sugar Ray upended the champion with one ferocious assault. At 2:51 of the second round, Olson was on the canvas and Sugar Ray once again middleweight champion of the world, once again the hottest attraction in boxing.

No one in ring history ever had scored a more dramatic personal triumph. And only Sugar Ray himself could accurately measure its scope. It had been the fight of his life. Not the Olson bout; that was only part of it. The whole comeback struggle—his financial disaster, his shattered pride and his fear of failure—stacked up bigger and was more terrifying than any opponent he had ever faced. The fight *outside* the ring was the toughest of all.

Sugar Ray's dramatic return began one day in the fall of 1954 when he announced he would box a six-round exhibition with Gene Burton in Ontario. It was to be a test-run for a possible full-blown comeback, he said. The announcement landed on the boxing world like an H-bomb. Some fight people weren't surprised. They had heard rumors of Sugar Ray's financial difficulties. But the average fan was completely dismayed. Robinson coming back! It was almost unbelievable. An old fighter doesn't hit the trail again unless he's pinched for dough. What happened to his bankroll, everybody wanted to know. What happened to the Harlem capitalist, the smart guy who had been sinking his big purses into solid business investments? One didn't have to tug at the memory to recall Sugar Ray's handsome, beaming face that December day only two years earlier, when he had announced his retirement. He was set up for life, he had said. It was no fairy tale. He had three apartment houses, a bar and grill, a barber shop, a dry-cleaning establishment, a lingerie shop, a real estate office and a few other minor interests. Dun and Bradstreet rated his holdings at $300,000. In addition, he was starting a lucrative career in show business, threatening to become one of the highest-paid dancing acts ever to hit the night-club circuit.

Ray had been held up as a sparkling example of the fight game, living proof that the popular notion that all fighters end up battered, senseless and broke wasn't so. He accepted the citation proudly. And why not? He had been a great fighter—the greatest of all, some said—and when he hung up his gloves he still had all his good looks, all his marbles and most of his money.

What had happened to spoil all this? Sugar Ray brushed aside all inquiries at the time, his immense pride shielding his many wounds. He was "investment poor," he explained. He needed "walking-around money." The explanation found few takers. And it wasn't until his comeback was successfully completed that Ray poured out all the details of his personal tragedy.

It is a fantastic story, a sad story that tugs at the heart. Even Sugar Ray becomes a little unwound retelling some of the more nightmarish chapters. He shakes his head in wonderment, still finding it hard to believe it happened to *him*. He stares at the floor, and when he looks up you notice that his eyes are damp.

He admits his mistakes. He admits that he wasn't the businessman he was cracked up to be. The problem began right there. He violated the cardinal rule of a new business—he took his eyes off the cash register. But he really didn't have a choice. His dancing act kept him on the move. He was booked into the best night clubs and theaters in the U.S. and Europe. His businesses were in New York City. There was only one solution; he had to let other people mind the store. "I picked out some people to run my affairs for me," Ray says. "They were people I had known for some time. They were competent and I felt I could trust them with important matters. I gave them my power of attorney to write checks and sign important papers. Just about everything was in their hands. And for two years I was led to believe that business was good. Then the roof fell in."

In September, 1954, Ray was in the midst of a triumphant tour of Europe with his dancing act when he received an urgent message from his secretary. His businesses were going to pot. He had better rush home.

Ray wasted no time canceling his tour and returning to the States. He found that all the enterprises which he had been assured were so secure were on the verge of crumbling. His real-estate holdings were about to be foreclosed. Uncle Sam was demanding delinquent tax payments. Bill collectors were kicking at the door. The books showed a staggering loss of more than $200,000, including about $50,000 from his hoofing engagements which he had poured into the businesses. On top of this it had cost him $20,000 to settle a suit lodged against him by a coal-delivery man who had been bitten by a dog belonging to one of Ray's employees. Sugar Ray's staff hadn't even bothered to protect him with insurance. The situation was terrifying. It placed Ray on the brink of complete financial disaster. The security he had accumulated carefully over 12 years through the sweat of his brow and the magic of his fists had vanished almost overnight.

The blow sent him reeling, but it was only the beginning of the mental punishment he was to encounter on the climb back up the hill. When he tried to pick up the pieces, he made another discovery that hit him even harder than the loss of his money.

"At a time like that a fellow just naturally looks for his friends," Ray explains sadly. "I thought I had made thousands of them during my fighting days. But how wrong I was! They weren't friends—they were just acquaintances. When I looked around for them, they weren't there. They didn't know me any more. I wasn't after their money. I needed advice—an honest opinion, someone to lean on for awhile, someone to pat me on the shoulder and tell me I'd make it. But I couldn't even get anyone to answer my telephone calls or my letters."

Robinson drops his head a little when he talks about one old friend, Walter Winchell, and makes no attempt to conceal what is an obvious wound. Before Sugar Ray's retirement, he and Winchell were warm friends. WW made him a member of the Damon Runyon Cancer Fund and Ray responded by donating the purses of three fights, totaling more than $100,000. Few fighters have displayed such generosity. Winchell told the world about it. He praised Sugar Ray at every turn, both in his syndicated column and over the radio. When Robinson reached his crisis, he turned to Winchell for advice.

"Like the others, he wasn't 'available' either!" Ray tells. "I only wanted a word with him—five minutes of his time. I never heard from him."

You begin to understand now what Ray means when he explains that his comeback wasn't launched merely for the money it would produce. To understand that, you have to appreciate what makes Robinson tick. You must measure his immense pride. Observe his swagger. He has always been a winner. The problem couldn't be solved with a loan or a pencil and a ledger. He had to show somebody something. He had to see what would happen if he got back on top again. As Ray put it, it was something he could do only inside the ring.

Sportswriters wept in print over his decision. Fighters who once had attempted the same treacherous path shook their heads mournfully. This writer was with Joe Louis the day Sugar Ray made the fateful announcement. The Bomber knew all about desperation comebacks—the risks, the futility, the humiliation. He knew Robinson, too. They were buddies. Both had sprung from Detroit's Black Bottom and together they had traveled many miles. The news touched him deeply. "What's the matter with that boy?" Joe said, fretfully. "Is he trying to get himself killed?"

After the dry-run with Burton, Robinson knocked out Joe Rindone in six on January 9, 1955, his first legitimate fight in 31 months. His critics were silent, but not for long. Ten days later, in a nationally-televised bout at Chicago Stadium, Tiger Jones, an in-and-outer at best, clouted Sugar Ray hard and often, and scored a decisive victory.

Now the chant became louder. Sportswriters dug into the cliche file and led off their columns with: "They never come back . . ." Open letters were written imploring Sugar Ray to give up his plan. Others even demanded that he retire. A campaign was launched to ban him from the ring in order to preserve his mental and physical well being— to prevent what seemed certain self-destruction. Robinson was stunned by it all.

"It was so hard to understand. How could so many

people really believe that I had lost it all?" Ray asked then, and still wonders now. "The same people who had said so many kind things about my fighting not too long before that! I couldn't believe that I was all through. And, yet, what was I to think? Was I right and everyone else wrong?"

This was the beginning of the long and difficult haul. There was trouble at every turn. Associates who had been with him since his early fighting days now departed, unwilling or unable to watch Ray prepare for a beating. When he tried to set up his training camp at Greenwood Lake, N. Y., after the Jones disaster, he could get no one to go with him. He brooded. He walked the floor. He had to take pills to get some sleep.

It was here that Ray's wife, Edna Mae, stepped in and took charge. She was the most important person in his corner. There were others—three to be exact. Joe Glaser, whose Associated Booking Corporation handled Robinson's dancing act; Ernie Braca, a well-heeled figure familiar on the boxing beat; and Harold Johnson, an ex-Harlem Globetrotter, were the others. They had helped him start the comeback by taking his mind off his pressing business problems. They told him what to do and assumed many burdens themselves. Glaser, alone, advanced Sugar Ray more than $90,000, saved his real estate from foreclosure and enabled his businesses to continue.

"They treated me like a son," Ray says. "They really saved me."

But it was Edna Mae, a beautiful former Cotton Club dancer to whom Ray has been married for almost 13 years, who took on the most important job in this crisis. By carefully analyzing every detail of the problem and explaining it convincingly, she bolstered Robinson's spirit and confidence at a time when he was very close to giving up.

"I had to believe her, because she was opposed to my comeback at the start," Robinson explains. "She wanted no part of it, and said there were other ways we could work the thing out. She even wanted to go back to work herself just to help out. Now she was telling me I had to go on. It was something I had to do—and do right—or I'd carry the scar of failure the rest of my life."

Edna Mae hammered away at the doubt that was giving Ray those sleepless nights, Robinson reveals. It was only man-made indecision, she insisted. And what did the sportswriters really know about it? Most of them had never been inside a prize ring. How could anyone flatly declare something to be impossible without knowing the size of a man's heart—or the faith contained therein? Edna told him it was time for him to display that faith—in himself and in God.

"Edna Mae's pep talks seemed to make sense," Ray says. "I thought about her arguments every minute I was alone. Why couldn't a champion fighter come back? When God put man on earth He didn't say: 'You can do this much and no more.' But there have always been skeptics. The history books are loaded with men who did the impossible—Ford, Edison, and the fellow who invented the steamboat, for instance. Nobody believed them—but they didn't lose faith in what they set out to do, did they?"

Deep now in prayer, and armed, he felt, with new spirit, Ray made another attempt at the steep hill. But after he could do no better than a split-decision win against Johnny Lombardo in Cincinnati, he faced still another crisis. His brain trust was ready to toss in the towel.

They told him it was all over. They would help him get on his feet, they said, and help him with his businesses. He wouldn't want for anything. It was the best way—to continue would only be dangerously foolhardy.

It was then that Sugar Ray had to make a confession. He told them about his training camp—or lack of it. How he couldn't get anyone to help him. He had no trainers, no sparring partners. Why, he hid to beg some lightweight he had met on the street one day to go to camp with him and box a few rounds. Sure it was embarrassing—the great Sugar Ray Robinson, the dandy of his day, begging people to go to camp with him. He hated to admit it but he had no choice. He was looking for one more chance.

"Help me set up a camp in the right way," he told them. "Help me get ready for one more fight properly. Then, if I don't do better, I'll do as you say—I'll hang them up for good."

The board of directors was startled. Perhaps it was the revelation of Ray's training problems. Or maybe it was Ray's insistence on one more fight his determination in face of the mounting odds. They relented. The camp was set up. Ray had his sparring partners, and everything else he needed to prepare for what easily could be his last fight.

After two hard months of training, Robinson met Ted Olla in April. The results were satisfactory; he stopped Olla in three. Two weeks later, he won a 10-round decision over Garth Panter.

Rocky Castellani was next. Rocky was the chief contender for Olson's middleweight crown, and he was a pretty fair hitter. Sugar Ray, having reached the second plateau, as they say on the quiz shows, wasn't going to let a title shot get away from him now. He went at the hard training grind for two solid months and when he met Castellani on July 22, all that hard work came to Robinson's rescue.

For five rounds Sugar Ray chased the back-peddling

Rocky, catching up with him often enough to gain a slight edge in points at the half-way mark. In the sixth round, Rocky put Robinson on the canvas, and the complexion of the fight changed immediately. Few fighters get off the floor to win—hardly any who are 35 years old. It takes them longer to recuperate. They have no reserve of stamina. When Sugar Ray fell the cry around ringside went up: "This is it."

Robinson had other ideas. He weathered the storm and came back like a tiger in the seventh to take the round by a wide margin. In the closing rounds, Sugar Ray picked his openings, more than held his own, and came off with a split-decision win. It was a courageous performance and it earned Ray the chance he had been working for—a shot at Olson and his old middleweight crown.

Throughout the comeback, Ray had tried desperately to determine precisely what it was that made it so difficult for an old fighter to climb back up those stairs. No one had to tell him he wasn't the Sugar Ray of yesterday. But why? He refused to concede that the passage of time had changed so many things. He was in shape. His punch was good. So were his legs. And he was determined. What was it that made him look so bad against fellows he could have taken apart only a short time before?

He got the answer one day while training for the Olson fight. "I was running along the road, moaning a little, thinking a little, when suddenly it hit me. I stopped in my tracks and cried out: 'Man, where is your skill?' Sure that was it—skill. I had been trying to kayo those fellows—win them big. And that wasn't my style of fighting. I was no knockout guy. I got to be champion by using my wits— by boxing." It was an important discovery. Thereafter, Ray began to recapture, more and more, the positive parts of his old ring style. That was really the beginning of the Robinson comeback.

Considering the second-round knockout of Olson, one might assume that Sugar Ray discarded his boxing skill for the fast, kayo punch—that he left his "important discovery" in the training camp. This wasn't so. Robinson says he used his wits to beat Olson. He set a trap for him, encouraged him to use his right hand, built up his confidence in that move. When Olson snapped at the bait, Sugar Ray unloaded. He wobbled Bobo in the first round. The next time he caught him, Olson hit the deck. Sugar Ray was home at last.

"It was impossible only because they *thought* it was impossible. I made it back because I thought it was possible and because it was something the Lord had directed me to do," Sugar Ray explains.

Many things have changed since Robinson battled his way back to the middleweight title. His old friends are tugging at his sleeve again. The telephone never stops ringing. Television and radio shows pursue him regularly for guest shots. A secretary has a full-time job acknowledging banquet invitations, requests for photographs and fan mail.

Robinson has changed, too. He is humble, leads a more conservative life. His entourage, once befitting a Roman emperor and including valets, barbers, chauffeurs, and housemen, no longer exists. He keeps close to his office by day and spends more time with Edna Mae and Ray, Jr., their six-year-old son.

What about the future? What's in it for Ray?

"This isn't a new career, believe me," Robinson points out. "I know that a fellow can go on just so long. I'm not kidding myself. Fighting is a tough business. Very frankly,

I've never loved it like most fighters do. I used to run away from violence when I was a kid. And I found it pretty hard to continue my career after Jimmy Doyle died a few hours after I knocked him out. I lost the killer instinct after that, and I fought just hard enough to win."

Right now Ray's future depends on his April 20 meeting with Bobo Olson in Los Angeles, when he puts his title on the line for the first time. Considering Robinson's 3-0 record against the ex-champion, there would appear to be little risk involved. Evidently the odds-makers do not agree. Shortly after Sugar Ray signed for the fight, the bookies established Olson as a 7-5 morning-line favorite.

Ray wasn't taking anything for granted. Late in January, he started his workouts in a Harlem gym, where he could stay close to his business office. In mid-February, he reopened his camp at Greenwood Lake, N.Y., and dug in for a long training grind.

While Robinson is hesitant about looking beyond the fight with Olson, it is no secret that his future plans center about a meeting with Carmen Basilio, the popular welterweight champion. This would be the big one—the money fight, the solution to many of Ray's financial problems. The IBC has it scheduled for June, possibly at Yankee Stadium, but it is likely that Robinson will ask to have it pushed back until September.

At any rate, Sugar Ray's boxing plans are limited to the next year. He'll be 36 years old on May 3. He has "young" legs and never has been bothered by a weight problem. Off his brief but brilliant assault on Olson, one might think he could go on indefinitely. Robinson is realistic, however, and so is his board of strategy. They are figuring on three more fights at the most. By that time, the rehabilitation of Sugar Ray's business interests should be complete. And since the planning now is being done more intelligently, Ray's financial structure ought to be much sounder than it was when he first retired in 1952.

Joe Glaser is the important man behind the program. He is a shrewd businessman. For 30 years he has helped the biggest name attractions of show business reap large rewards for their talents. His office handles more than 500 artists, including Louie Armstrong, Noel Coward, Duke Ellington, Dorothy Lamour, Errol Flynn, Woody Herman and Lionel Hampton. His friendship with Robinson covers more than 15 years, although they have been associated in business for only the last five. Glaser booked Sugar Ray's dancing act into the big entertainment spots, and got him some very fancy prices for his dancing. Robinson earned as much as $15,000 a week. No dancer, Glaser claims, has ever approached that figure—not even the great Bill (Bojangles) Robinson.

Ray's managers of record are Ernie Braca and Harold Johnson. George Gainford, identified as Robinson's manager through most of his career and credited with discovering Ray in the amateur ranks, still works in the corner but his role has changed considerably. Actually, Gainford never received the "manager's cut" of Robinson's purses over the years for the simple reason that Ray was his own boss and made his own deals. There was a falling out between the two after Robinson retired, but that has been patched up and Sugar Ray is sentimental about the presence of Gainford and trainer Harry Wiley in his corner. Both have been with him through all his fights.

Braca and Johnson sit in on all important consultations, but it is Glaser who is the strong man. He is the one Jim Norris and other promoters must deal with. Robinson refuses to sign or agree to anything without getting Joe's formal approval. He remembers too well the disastrous aftermath of his last disagreement with Glaser. That was prior to the Tiger Jones fight. Ray thought Jones was a suitable opponent, and so did Gainford. Glaser screamed a warning and when it was rejected he came very close to ending his ties with Sugar Ray. The outcome of the fight substantiated Glaser's judgment and actually strengthened the association of the two men.

Glaser reveals that great strides have been made in the rehabilitation program. The tax lien of $81,000, slapped on Robinson by the federal government, has been substantially reduced. The purse for the up-coming Olson fight—Robinson has a $75,000 guarantee against a percentage—should do much to place Sugar Ray's affairs in good order. And Glaser expects to liquidate most of Robinson's businesses within the next 30 days. This would include the bar and grill, dry-cleaning store, etc.—but not Ray's real estate holdings. The stores are good investments, but they depend on Robinson being there. He can't just leave his name on the door and expect booming business.

There are other big plans for the future. Robinson is preparing to write his life story, and Glaser already has a "solid" offer of $250,000 from Hollywood for the movie rights. Ray's appearance on "Omnibus," the television show, in which he showed himself to be a glib and polished performer, started another wave of "feelers" for possible future work in that field.

Sugar Ray isn't thinking about his retirement plan at the moment. Not while he has that date with Olson. But when he does finally hang up the gloves for keeps, his place among the all-time greats of the game will be dusted off and waiting for him.

Arnold Palmer's Playing A Hot Hand

In golf, 1955 is notable as the year that relative unknown Jack Fleck, in perhaps golf's biggest upset, defeated Ben Hogan in a playoff to win the U.S. Open. But a victory of greater historical significance had occurred earlier that summer when the Canadian Open was won by a brash PGA rookie named Arnold Palmer. It was Palmer's first professional victory and it launched a career that would revolutionize the sport. Before he was through, Palmer would rack up 61 PGA wins, including seven Major Championships, but, more significantly, by his swashbuckling style and charismatic ways, Palmer provided the impetus to transform golf into a multi-billion dollar industry. When Jack Zanger filed this report in 1958, following Palmer's first Masters victory, the author sensed a brazen quality in Palmer that foretold a special future—but he had no idea just how special it would become. Nobody did.

By Jack Zanger
September 1958

IT MAY BE that the writers who cover the professional golf circuit started it in their constant search for angles, but the story persists nonetheless that Arnold Palmer cares only about winning, not about making money. Taken one way, this has the happy sound of the true professional, disregarding all for the sake of the pure joy of competition. But then there is the other side—the insinuation that if he finds himself in a position where he can't take it all, Palmer picks up his ball and goes home. This, the attitude suggests, is unsportsmanlike.

Palmer once said, on this subject: "I'm in this game to win titles. Money is not the biggest factor. I want to be the best—the Masters champion, the Open champion, the PGA champion." To swallow that statement down to the last chew, you would have to be just as willing to believe that General Motors only wants to make the finest cars on the road, not to earn handsome dividends.

What is good for General Motors is good for Arnold Palmer. It is true enough that Palmer cares heavily about winning the big titles. But the same can be said for almost anyone who plays golf for a living. Palmer wants the prestige and the lasting fame, to be sure, but he does not show contempt for the money that comes along. What has created the impression that he "goes for broke" is simple enough: He has one of the soundest games in golf, he has won nine major tournaments in three years (more than any other golfer has won over the same stretch) and, as a consequence, he can afford to entertain lofty ambitions.

"All this talk about Palmer just being out for the glory is hokum," says Gene Sarazen, himself the winner of two Opens, three PGA titles and one Masters, among other baubles. "Sure, I'll go along that he wants to win the big ones, to prove he's the best. Who doesn't? But remember this. It's the big ones like the Open and the PGA that are the big money tournaments, too. The others, the regular weekly shows, are strictly cash-and-carry. The real money is in the big ones. And anyone who says he isn't in this game for the money is crazy."

But great golfers, Sarazen believes, truly are motivated more by pride than the promise of financial gain. "I don't think you could buy Ben Hogan's victory in the British Open for $50,000," he says. "Ben wanted to prove he was just as good in England's backyard as he was here. Today's golfer isn't out to conquer, not the way Hogan was, or Walter Hagen. Today they play with cash registers in their heads. What we need today are more conquerors, more players like Palmer."

Palmer joined the tour in 1955, two months after he had won the National Amateur, and he displayed, in the beginning, a brash win-or-else attitude. If he found, in an early round or at any time, that he was pretty much out of it, he would quit. At the Cavalcade of Golf, he shot a 78 in the first round and withdrew from the tourney. In the Mayfair Inn Open, he fired a 72 for the first 18 holes. Again he pulled out. Then, in 1956, at the Motor City Open in Detroit, he had a 77 after the opening round, and was on his way out of town by nightfall.

None of these walkaways delighted the other pros. They rubbed against accepted golf protocol. You can't win them all, the familiar cliché goes, and you ought to hang in there.

Besides, walking out on a tourney doesn't sit well with the galleries, or with the tournament director. Recently, the PGA passed a rule fining a golfer $100 if he walks out during a tourney.

"What's wrong with pulling out of a tournament if your game is going sour?" Sarazen asks. "Doesn't a manager take out a pitcher when he doesn't have his stuff? Arnie is a title player, and that's a rare thing in golf today. Cary Middlecoff is the same way, and Doug Ford would be, too, if he had the swing. He's got the determination and the ability to be a big winner. But Arnie has the swing—and everything else. No wonder he wants to win as many titles as he can. There's nothing wrong with his attitude. Sure, he's in a minority, but the crowd loves a fellow who plays boldly, who won't settle for second place. The guys who play it safe and try just to finish in the money would be happy running a grocery store in a small town."

Arnold Palmer is a sinewy, almost pugnacious looking young man who barely took time to make a few friends when he joined the pro circuit before he began picking up the pay checks. "I was brought up on a golf course," he says. "It gave me a big advantage." His father, Millard Palmer, has been the pro at the Latrobe (Pa.) Country Club since 1921.

"When I first joined the tour," Palmer says, "I used to get disgusted when I didn't play well. If I felt I couldn't win, I'd say the hell with it and walk off. But I wouldn't do that today. I don't know what changed my attitude. It just changed. Now I'm interested in my scoring average and how I finish. I don't walk off any more."

None of this, however, has altered Arnie's attitude about winning. "Sure I'm interested in making money," he says. "That's my livelihood, after all. But I'm more interested in winning the big titles. I want to be a great player."

There is little difference, Palmer claims, between winning a weekly ham-and-egger and taking a major title. They are all tough. When he first went on the tour, his aim was to win a tournament—any tournament. Then, after a while, the weekly invitationals began to look less exciting. "The competition is just as tough,"

Palmer explains, "but after you've won one of them, and then two or three, they get to feel the same. You find yourself pointing for the big ones. It's like winning your maiden. You seem to step up in class. That's what winning the Masters felt like."

What about second place? "If I can't win, I'd just as soon settle for third place. By that I mean that I'll always try to win as long as I have a chance, knowing that if I miss I'm just as willing to take third as second. I don't think I gamble as much as I once did, but you might say that experience has taught me when to play boldly and when not to."

Arnie never wanted to be anything but a tournament golfer. "Before I was five, my father taught me the way to grip a club. This, I think, is the most important fundamental in golf." When he grew older, Arnie caddied on the local golf course and became good enough to beat the other caddies regularly. He won a flock of western Pennsylvania junior titles, and at Wake Forest College, he took the Atlantic Coast Conference title three out of four years (he was runnerup the other time). He spent three years in the Coast Guard before finishing his education in June, 1954.

Three months later, Arnie was the U.S. Amateur champion. Having reached the climax to an amateur golfer's dream, he took the step he had been preparing for all his life. He turned professional in November and became a regular member of the tour the following spring. Although he had to wait out the mandatory six-month period before he was eligible to accept prize money, Arnie played well enough in the early tournaments to indicate he would make a good living out of the game. He took home his first pay check ($145) when he tied for 25th place in the Fort Wayne Open. He made his biggest bite by winning the Canadian Open, worth $2,400 in first-prize money. His earnings for the year came to $7,958.32 for 32nd place.

Despite a spotty performance record in 1956, Arnie climbed to 19th place, with $16,144.66. He led the circuit in tournament victories with four—the Panama Open ($2,000), the Columbia Open ($1,800), the Insurance City Open ($4,000) and the Eastern Open ($3,800). Last year, he again led with four tournament wins (the Houston, Azalea, Rubber City and San Diego Opens) and raised his winnings to $27,802.80 for fifth place.

"He's never really had much trouble with his temper—not since he was in high school," his father says. "And when he did in those days, I told him he would have to put a stop to it. When things didn't go well on the tour, he'd come home for a rest, and we'd try to iron out any rough spots."

Actually, Arnie and his father agree about everything when it comes to golf, except his putting. Millard Palmer favors—and teaches—a more sweeping movement while putting, but Arnie likes to crack his wrists when he's lining one up. But it is on the tee and on the fairways, where a long iron will get him home, that Arnie's game is strongest. A robust 5-11, weighing 180 pounds, he is only a few yards behind George Bayer and Paul Harney, the acknowledged longest hitters in golf. Short chips occasionally give him trouble, and he used to change putters frequently. "I used to think it was the putter's fault when they didn't drop," he says, "but I've got away from that. I still change putters occasionally, but only because I want a certain putter for a certain green. And then I'll generally go back to the putter I've been using most of the time. But I don't think my putting is as good now as it was years ago."

Aside from his Masters triumph this April, Arnie won the St. Petersburg Open earlier in the year. "Look over my record lately," he said after the Masters, "and you'll see that I haven't finished out of the money very often. In fact, I've generally been coming in 12th or better." Including his $11,250 check for winning at Augusta, Arnie's earnings up to that point were $19,883.33, which put him in first place on the tour.

Claude Harmon thinks Arnie's accurate long driving has been the key to his success so far, and he believes it is bound to continue. "He's a long hitter," Harmon says. "He practices eight hours a day and he has callouses on his hands that are big enough for you to light matches off."

Just before the Open at the Southern Hills course in Tulsa, Okla., last June, somebody asked Arnie which of the major titles meant the most to him. "I wouldn't know about that," he said. "Winning the Masters was my biggest thrill, and not having won the Open, I couldn't truthfully say which one would mean the most to me. If I ever win the Open, ask me then."

He can be sure somebody will.

Pancho Gonzalez:
All Dressed Up And
Nowhere To Play

In the summer of 1955 Pancho Gonzalez was recognized as the world's No. 1 tennis player and among the top players of all time. But he was a professional at a time when amateurism ruled at Grand Slam tournaments and when the American pro game was in disarray. Among the pros of the mid 1950s, Gonzalez had no peers, regularly beating the likes of Don Budge, Bobby Riggs and Pancho Segura in challenge matches as they roamed gypsie-like across the nation. But by 1955 the American public had tired of their barnstorming tours. With open competition still 13 years away, Al Stump recounts how these factors conspired to force Gonzalez, 26 and at the peak of his talent, to ponder his future.

By Al Stump
August 1955

HERE IS A STRANGE and sorry thing: For more than a year now, one of the world's foremost athletic champions has faced a career blackout. He stands among the all-time greats of his calling—yet he has no audience. At 26, he is no less a genius in his field than are Eddie Arcaro, Otto Graham, Stan Musial or Ben Hogan in theirs. But the hall is dark; the crowd is gone.

Pancho Gonzalez, the best tennis player in the world today, is all dressed up with no place to go. The decay and collapse of American professional tennis leaves the gamemaster no place in this country to express his talent or to earn a living with it. Worse, there seems little or no chance for a comeback of the pro game.

What—at the peak of his abilities—is there for the big, handsome Latin who struggled from the wrong side of the tracks to the top of the tennis world, to do? How does he bear his frustration? SPORT has sought to find out . . .

His friends say that Ricardo Alonzo Gonzalez is a troubled man. As a boy growing up on the teeming south side of Los Angeles, he developed the most powerful service since Bill Tilden by tirelessly banging an old tennis ball off the wall of his father's garage. Today Pancho and Henrietta Gonzalez and their three children, Richard, Jr., six, Mike, five, and Danny, four, live at 5839 South Arlington Avenue, in an average-income Los Angeles, residential district, in a one-story, two-bedroom house they bought for less than $12,000 six years ago. It is not the home you'd expect of a colorful star who won two U.S. amateur championships and earned more than $150,000 between 1950 and 1954 on the national professional circuit. It is the home of a man determined to hang onto what he has.

The Gonzalez cottage has a garage, containing a new-model Mercury family sedan. Sometimes, in the mornings, neighbors hear the *spat* of a ball bounding and rebounding off the back wall of the garage. "Pancho," they say wryly, "is practicing."

More often, though, you'll find the idle champion passing the time in a small, wired-in dog run he has constructed in the rear of his yard. He has become a breeder, in a modest way, of pedigreed boxers. His favorite is Bruno, a brawny, beige-colored male of 75 pounds he bought in London in 1950. Duchess, a fine female, has delivered three litters for breeder Gonzalez, with the pups selling for from $75 to $125. It is a bad joke, of course, but Pancho, in the unrest of his inactivity, remarks that maybe all those wisecracks about tennis bums aren't so wrong. "Look at me," he has said. "I've gone to the dogs."

Ten blocks from Pancho's home is the Twentieth Century Recreation Bowl. Nobody in the bowling alley knows a volley from a lob, or cares that Jack Kramer, the former world pro champion, now admits he no longer can beat Gonzalez, or that Australia's Frank Sedgman was swept off the court by Gonzalez, 21 matches to nine, in a tour of Australia and the Orient two winters ago. They only recognize the lean, six-foot three-inch, 190-pounder as a tough guy to bowl against in a "pot game" (for modest stakes). Three nights a week, Pancho and "Henry," his wife, roll in a recreation league. It is something to do.

"This Gonzalez, I don't know anything about his other game," says Charley Peroni, a high-average rec bowler and teacher, "but he could be another Varipapa at this one if he worked at it. I've seen him bowl at least 75 games of 240 pins or more. Just foolin' around, he has a 183 average. Some of the sharpest shooters in town hang out here and this Gonzalez cleans 'em out in pot games . . . he's got that great wrist action."

Excessive bowling stiffened Pancho's wrist to the point that he was hitting awkward backhands in the World Professional Championship Tournament last year at Los Angeles—the one major appearance available to him in the U.S. in 1954. Nevertheless, he handled Sedgman with ease in the semi-finals, 7-5, 6-3, 6-4. In the final, Pancho Segura, a two-time pro champ, carried him to the fifth set before Gonzalez proved again he is the best in the business.

If there is one thing that characterizes Gonzalez, it is his steady yearning for competition. As a 15-year-old at Manual Arts High School in Los Angeles, he was matched in a quarter-mile race with trackmen two years older. Pancho's thin legs pumped around the track. He fell across the tape—and collapsed. But he won—in 52 seconds flat. Now he takes out his suppressed energy by knocking down ten pins.

Clutching at odd forms of expression is something Pancho has been doing since pro tennis first began to slip in late 1953. Then, and in early '54, the last of a series of Jack Kramer-promoted barnstorming tours slumped about 50 per cent at the box office. The year Pancho turned pro, 1949, 18,000 people packed Madison Square Garden to watch Kramer duel Gonzalez. Pancho earned a record $5,400 for that night's work. Last year, the Garden draw was 4,300 people. In many major cities as few as 400 fans showed up. Of the over-all $125,000 gross, the troupe of Gonzalez, Sedgman, Segura and Don Budge lost money for their backers. There will be no 1955 tour—and none is foreseen for 1956. The pros, in short, seem finished.

"Old-timers like me and Bobby Riggs and Budge aren't hurt by the bust-up," says the 34-year-old Kramer, bothered with an arthritic back and now in the golf-course business. "But Pancho is young, at the top of his game—maybe the best singles player who ever lived. For him to be sidelined is a shame."

Instead of displaying his talents before enthusiastic

tennis crowds these days, Pancho is apt to be in the town of Saugus, Calif., 40 miles north of Los Angeles, where he'd look very odd carrying a tennis racquet. Saugus, with one of the fastest "drag strips" in the area, is the roaring, oil-spattered scene of jalopy, roadster and stock car racing. One morning in early spring an interviewer found Pancho sitting on an overturned fuel can at the strip. Pancho wore clean, white garageman's coveralls and heavy boots. A crash helmet was perched on the back of his curly black hair. In his slow, quiet way, he was talking about what brought him to Saugus.

"I was never one of those hot-rod punks who drive the cops crazy," he said. "It was the mechanical end I liked. Maybe you remember those stories about me getting kicked out of high school three or four times? Once they barred me from junior tennis for a year because I was a truant. Well, I wasn't always off hitting balls. I'd find some kid who owned an old clunker—never could afford one myself—and I'd tear it down and put it together.

"I'm a good grease-monkey," he said seriously.

Lately, he explained, he'd been keeping busy behind a racing wheel. He owned his own car—a low-slung, white-painted, stripped-down coupe parked nearby. "We go today," he said. "Stick around."

A chunky man in an official timer's cap walked up. He studied Gonzalez. "You going to be the chauffeur this afternoon? Or you going to be smart?"

Gonzalez nodded. "I'm driving. Maybe I'll blow higher'n a kite, though. There's something wrong with the fuel intake."

"You have a shield behind the fire wall?"

"Oh, sure."

(A few weeks earlier, a drag-stripper's clutch had

blown up at 100-plus miles per hour, the car overturned, fire engulfed the cockpit and the driver was burned to death. Most of the Saugus irons now have both an asbestos firewall and a steel clutch plating between engine and driver.)

A garage-owner chum of Pancho's named Bob Duncan was tuning up the coupe. Occasionally, he drives for Gonzalez. As Duncan depressed the accelerator, it reached a high shrieking whine. The timing boss wagged his head in a baffled way before moving off.

"Why does he do it?" he muttered to nobody in particular. "A million dollar athlete—and he's out here risking a broken arm. Or neck."

Gonzalez is a sober, reflective type. But now he said laughingly, "Everybody tells me that. They think I'm absolutely crazy. But this drag racing isn't dangerous . . . ."

Duncan looked up. "Yeah—unless a tire blows. Or something breaks."

The compact power plant in which Pancho has invested several thousand dollars is no toy. Beneath the 1934 Ford chassis is a 1951 eight-cylinder Cadillac engine hyped to 375 horsepower. It can go 160 mph on the straightway, or only 20 mph less than most Indianapolis 500-mile cars at top speed. However, drag events aren't conducted like an Indianapolis race. The start is from a standstill. At the flag's drop, cars are kicked into a zooming getaway. In a straight rush down a converted airplane landing strip, the idea is to reach the finish line a quarter-mile away at the highest possible acceleration. That morning at Saugus, Pancho had hit 109.6 mph when he flashed past the timing lights. It was one of the two fastest times in his class of 18 entrants and put him in the finals. He was matched against the drag champ from Pomona, Calif. The prize—a trophy worth about $3.

"They'd never know you at Forest Hills now," a bystander commented.

"They wouldn't know me anyway," Pancho replied. "They cancelled the pro championship matches out of Forest Hills two years ago. We're prophets without honor."

A crowd of perhaps 2,500 watched the race. The coupes' pick-up was amazing: in less than 500 feet they were moving at 70 mph. At 1,000 feet, the racers were bumper-to-bumper. Near the finish, the Pomona pilot slewed on the oily asphalt and seemed about to sideswipe Gonzalez. The speed now was about 110 mph. But he straightened out—and in that instant, Pancho gained a three-foot margin. He won by about that much.

"See? Nothing to it," he said to the worried Duncan, when he had braked in the pits. He caught the expression on his interviewer's face. "Well, I've got to do something, don't I? I like this. It's fun—and just risky enough."

One of Pancho's fingernails was smashed and swollen. He had dropped a heavy motor part on it a week earlier. On the back of the same right hand—his racquet hand— a white scar showed. He had cut it to the bone in a garage accident. Asked if he wasn't afraid a bad injury could cost him his deft touch on the tennis court, he shrugged. "Worry never solved anything."

After he had washed up, Pancho ate a thick steak at a Highway 99 drive-in and drove back to Los Angeles. There was another drag race in two weeks at Santa Ana. He said that in the meantime he would stick around the house mostly, give his oldest boy, Dick, Jr., tennis lessons, tend his dogs, go bowling and watch television. It had been two months since he had faced a top-flight opponent across the net. And then it was in exhibition. "I'd had hopes for a South American tennis series this summer," he mentioned on the way home, "It fell through—lack of promotion, I guess. Maybe I'll get to Europe later this year. It's up in the air right now. I can't tell you exactly why. All I know is that pro tennis is a dead duck."

What about an Open tennis championship, joining the amateurs and pros, as has been often suggested? "It'll happen some day. Not in the next five years, though," he said. "If an amateur won the Open, he'd turn pro for the money immediately. The Lawn Tennis Association crowd doesn't want that. If a pro beat the amateur champ, that would hurt amateur gates. Anyway, the people in charge figure we contaminate their boys. They'd like us to drop dead. Which we have."

Most critics believe the American public isn't tired of Gonzalez; only disinterested in the same old, inadequate faces who oppose him. Sedgman, the 1952 Wimbledon victor and two-time U.S. singles champion, only looked like Pancho's equal. Gonzalez's power, net-rushing and tremendous defensive coverage gave him a 32-18 edge in matches. When he lost, it appeared to many he was loafing. Jack Kramer has played his last serious match, and also may be through as a promoter. Bobby Riggs and Budge can't take a set from Pancho when he is bearing down. Ken McGregor of Australia, likewise. That leaves Pancho Segura, the gamest little man since Bitsy Grant. Now and then—as in the National Pro Open finals of 1951—Segura has pinned Gonzalez' ears back. But the 140-pound Ecuadorian no longer can run with Gonzalez or handle the service that becomes mightier each year, and Little Pancho sadly admits their long rivalry is too lopsided to keep the interest of demanding American fans. He beat Segura again last winter in the pro championships at Cleveland.

The idea, recently considered by pro promoters, of developing a Gonzalez opponent from among the world's four leading amateurs—Vic Seixas, Tony Trabert, Lew Hoad and Ken Rosewall—is a straw none are quite willing to grasp. "We might kid the customers for a few weeks," testifies Kramer, "but after that we'd have to make Gonzalez hit every shot off his backhand to keep it halfway even. Vic and Tony couldn't beat Segura—let alone Gonzalez. Hoad and Rosewall, both around 20 years old, might give Pancho an argument in three years. Right now, he'd ruin their pride. It would be a massacre."

If it's any comfort to "Gorgo"—the pro trade's nickname for Gonzalez, meaning "gorilla"—he has done what a rare few performers have accomplished. Like Joe Louis, Bobby Jones, Willie Hoppe and Man o' War before him, he has run out of competition.

The result has become so incongruous as to be pathetic. Two years ago, Pancho briefly experimented with a business career. He opened "Pancho's Tennis Shop" near the Exposition Park public courts in Los Angeles where he first learned the game. The store had a run of popularity. Then, realizing he had neither the interest in nor the knack for running a store, he sold out. He went only through the eleventh grade in school. The normal commercial outlets are blocked to him. "Figures aren't for Richard," says his wife, Henrietta, a petite, pretty brunette. "He is only really happy on the court."

When Kramer abandoned all touring activity this year, Pancho turned to golf. Frank Parker and Riggs introduced him to the game in 1950. In his first round he shot a 108 over the Augusta Masters course. He has never seen a sport he couldn't master and this spring Pancho put together a 75 on the difficult Inglewood, Calif., layout. About the time friends were urging him to copy Ellsworth Vines, who switched from tennis to big-time golf stardom, Pancho showed up in a semi-pro basketball tournament at Whittier, Calif. He was pretty good. As with golf, however, it was merely something to fill in a dull void.

His heart is in one place only: tennis.

Beyond idleness, another difficulty exists for Pancho. In society-controlled tennis, Pancho never has felt fully at ease. Early in his career he was unfairly made to seem crude and illiterate by class-conscious tennis sponsors. Even after he defeated Eric Sturgess and Ted Schroeder for the amateur titles in 1948 and 1949, there were insults and snubs. Pancho is sensitive. At one period he disappeared for two months, and not even his wife saw him. The passage of time has made Pancho poised and personable. He knows the right fork now. Yet hobnobbing with millionaires and diamond-dripping dowager patrons of the game isn't his idea of fun. Pancho has dropped most of his country-club connections since turning pro in 1949. So, at times, astonishingly, the world's top player has had trouble finding a place to work out.

One morning the past spring, a bunch of kids were swatting balls on a public playground near the Los Angeles Coliseum. The court had broad cracks in it and the net sagged. The kids gasped when a tall, wide shouldered figure in white shorts and T-shirt came through a side gate.

"Anybody want a game?" Pancho asked. For the next hour, the kids had the thrill of their lives slamming their best spins and chops at the pro champion. They ran him all over the place. Pancho went home sweaty and happy.

Los Angeles Tennis Club, which is less interested in social activities than it is in developing young talent, recently took Pancho off the hook. He can work there—at no charge—whenever he likes. "That doesn't solve his problem," says George Toley, the LATC pro. "There isn't anybody at the club who can give him a contest. You watch him playing pit-pat with the best amateurs in town, and you wonder how long he can hold his great game together."

An obvious outlet for his penned-in energy is instructing. The going rate of teaching pros on the Coast is $10 an hour. Gonzalez could make triple that amount. One of his friends reveals, "A movie producer tried to hire Pancho at a fantastic fee as his private coach. The guy was fat, 50 and swung like an old woman. He was the kind of guy a lot of pros out here live off of—like Bill Tilden did before he died."

Thus far Gonzalez hasn't yielded to this easy temptation. He hasn't taken on one film personality as a pupil, nor any other person who would subsidize him. "It's not my field," he says.

Instead, he stages regular teen-age clinics on public courts all around town, gives exhibitions for charity and tours homes for problem boys. Perry Jones, the "czar" of amateur tennis in Southern California, says an idle Gonzalez also is the best asset he has in maintaining the country's largest flow of junior titleholders. "Things like this happen all the time," explains Jones. "We had a terrific 16-year-old champion who was about to give up tennis. Same old reason—the football crowd at school told him he was playing a sissy game. I asked Pancho to take over. Well, when he walked out on the court at the boy's school—a big, hairy-legged fellow who hit the ball until it screamed—you should have seen the reaction. Now, half the kids there want to slug a ball like Pancho does."

Nevertheless, Pancho doesn't enjoy teaching. If Bobo Olson was forced to spend his days in a gym, showing young pugs how to hook a right hand; if Eddie Mathews was given nothing to do but show rookies how he hits home runs, they, too, would squirm uncomfortably.

"I wouldn't be at all surprised if he left this country for good," a source close to Pancho says. "We're liable to lose him to Australia."

Taxes and the drain of a large family have cut heavily into Gonzalez's savings. In addition, several years ago, on the advice of Seymour Greenberg, a Chicago amateur and financial expert, Gonzalez stripped himself of ready cash by investing a large sum in annuities. These will pay off years hence when his three boys are of college age. "The future is okay," he says. "Right now I need money."

The one place in the world where he knows he can earn it is in tennis booming Australia. Last September, shut out at home, he spent two months there, with astonishing results. Playing Sedgman, McGregor and Segura, he smashed attendance records from Melbourne to Perth to Adelaide to White City to Newcastle. The first three tourneys drew $66,000. Besides a percentage guarantee, Pancho was shooting for a 1,000-pound ($2,800) prize for each tourney he won. Before an average house of 10,000 Aussie fans, he whipped Sedgman 16 matches to nine, McGregor 15 matches to zero and Segura four matches to two.

In Perth, Sedgman had him match point in the fifth set. From the net, the local hero drove a smoking placement deep into the corner. It looked impossible to return. Diving into the crowd, Pancho flicked with the tip of his racquet. The ball lobbed high over Sedgman's head and dropped in, leaving Frank standing in rooted amazement. Gonzalez went on to crack Sedgman's game wide open and win. Perth fans stood and cheered the American for minutes. Later, Pancho couldn't get through his hotel lobby. It was jammed with Aussies whose appreciation of tennis artistry is everything that the present U.S. attitude is not.

Adding receipts from a swing northward to Tokyo and Manila, Pancho earned about $30,000 (less taxes) in four months. He was personally greeted by the Crown Prince of Japan. Philippine newspapers ran his picture in four columns on page one. In Seoul, Korea, 15,000 fans stood in a ticket line for hours to see him perform. Returning by airliner to Los Angeles, Pancho found not one reporter to meet him. There was a brief sports-page notice that he had returned from a Pacific tour. Then blackout.

Ricardo Alonzo Gonzalez, with all his honors, is not a happy man. Twenty-six is a beginning age for a professional. In any other field he would be at the crest of popularity and enjoying all the rewards. He has fought his way past the obstacles of poverty, race prejudice and the hostility of amateur tennis and gone on to dominate on a broader, more difficult stage. Pride, determination and hard work took him to the top. He is everything you look for in the American success story.

But there apparently is no future for him in tennis in America. Nobody knows where his story will end. But if we lose him to foreign soil, it won't be because he wants to go. It will be because he got a strange rap from fate— a champion with no place to play.

Why Bill Vukovich Has To Win The Indy 500

Bill Vukovich, a racing superstar in his era, arrived at the Brickyard in 1955 intent on becoming the first driver to win three consecutive Indy 500s. At 35, he seemed to have the right mix of experience and nerve to succeed. Instead, holding the lead on lap 57, he crashed and died. Death was a fate all too common among drivers of Vukovich's generation—26 of his racing buddies had died before him. But, prior to his final race, Vukovich had never suffered so much as a scratch in a major event. The following article by Al Stump hit the newsstands shortly before Vukovich waved to his wife and climbed into a car for the final time. In addition to providing fascinating insight into Vukovich— describing the intensity and aloofness that kept him out of racing's inner circle—it addresses with an eerie candor Vukovich's thoughts on mortality. Stump's story is followed by an editorial from SPORT *in which the editors call for the Indy 500 to be abolished.*

BY AL STUMP
JUNE 1955

AN ANNOUNCER, as excited as everyone else who saw Bill Vukovich drive to his second straight 500-mile triumph last June, worked his way through the crowded Victory Lane at the Indianapolis Speedway. He thrust a microphone in front of Vukovich.

"Here's a driver we'll never forget," he shouted. "Today he ranks with racing's immortals, with Ted Horn, Ralph Hepburn, Rex Mays, Wilbur Shaw, Chet Miller . . . ."

Vukovich, a small, tense, expressionless man with moody black eyes, pulled back sharply. "I don't like that immortal stuff," he said. Turning, he bluntly walked away from the interview.

Probably a good many people believed that the chunky Californian was living up to his famous reputation for being temperamental—if not eccentric. A better explanation for his action is that immortality is a status usually awarded posthumously in racing, and Vukovich is extremely sensitive to any suggestion that his life span may be short. Particularly so in this case—since Horn, Hepburn, Mays and Miller all died in bloody track crashes. "Vukie is a nice, likeable guy," says a former associate of his. "But he lives every day in the present. In his business, you can't afford to think about the future."

Age 35, Vukovich is a nontalkative Serbian-American who shot out of the unknown ranks in 1952 to become, today, the hottest driver in America. But the strain clearly shows. Since 1947, when he was competing in midget auto and roadster racing only, 26 drivers who were friends of Vukovich have been killed in action. Another of his buddies was retired with terrible burns. One has no left hand. Another is legless. A fourth is hopelessly paralyzed from the waist down.

Vukie, himself, creaks when he sits down. Skidding out of control during last November's Pan-American Road Race for stock cars in Mexico, he hurtled end-over-end off a mountain curve into a 50-foot canyon. "They welded my cracked vertebrae," he says, "but it still hurts whenever I'm off my feet."

"Miraculous" escapes are a dime a dozen in auto racing but Vukie holds one record he has every intention of prolonging: a 17-year cockpit veteran, he's never been hurt, never even scratched in big-car competition. Midget auto officials in California once threatened to bar him for hell-bent tactics which busted up Vukie in numerous places. Yet in the faster AAA sprint-car and Indianapolis major-car events he graduated to late in his career, he's led a charmed life.

With his rabbit's foot securely tied around his neck, the muscular, olive-skinned little man from Fresno, California, will be back at Motor Speedway for the 500-miler this coming Memorial Day to prove his record is no fluke. He hopes to improve that record and, in so doing, make racing history. Only the late Wilbur Shaw, in 1939-40, Mauri Rose in 1947-48 and Vukovich in 1953-54 have won two consecutive 500-milers. To be the first three-time repeater in the 43 years of the race is important to Vukie. He has a score to settle. He wants to silence the critics who insist that he doesn't belong with the all-time greats of the motordromes.

Last June, Vukovich drove a roadster-type Fuel Injection Engineering Special, owned by California oil millionaire Howard Keck, to a new 500-mile average-speed record of 130.840 mph. This despite a dust storm which for six and a half minutes put the field under the yellow "slow down" signal. The year before, a heat wave sent the track temperature to 130 degrees. One driver, Ray Scarborough, died of heat prostration; only six men drove the 500 miles without relief. Vukovich was one of them. He led on 195 of the 200 laps, three shy of Billy

Arnold's all-time record. "The finest driving I've ever seen," said Tommy Milton, 1921, '23 Indianapolis winner, now a dean of AAA officials. "I have to say that Vukovich is the greatest ever to perform on the Speedway."

Elsewhere, however, reservations were held. Some of the event's Old Guard had praise only for Keck's $35,000 Offenhauser-powered Special. Anybody could have won in the car, several track officials stated. In Los Angeles, where Vukie has tiffed with newspapermen, a headline read last June 1: "GREAT PIT CREW KEY TO VUKOVICH VICTORY." Fast work by his mechanics in getting Vukie back on the track was claimed to be his margin over second-place Jimmy Bryan of Phoenix and the close-up third finisher, Jack McGrath of Pasadena.

Still another sore spot with Vukie is the 500-miler of 1952—the catastrophe they won't let him forget. That year, at the 191-lap mark, he was whining along with a 19-second lead over Troy Ruttman. Only nine more times around the asphalt-and-brick course and he'd get the checkered victory flag. Suddenly Vukie seemed to lose control of his car. It fishtailed, slamming the wall at the northeast turn, rebounding, and striking again and again. Dazed but unhurt, Vukie jumped out, leaped the wall as Ruttman's bright thunderbolt passed. Why did Vukie "blow it" when he had the purse won? Because— some experts said—the relentlessly pressing Ruttman strained his nerves to the breaking point and, in trade lingo, he "geeked out."

"That's a lie," Vukovich says hotly. "The steering pin broke me. We invited everybody to take a look, but a lot of those guys don't like me for another reason. The reason is, I don't make them any money."

This refers to another highly touchy situation Vukie has created. Since 1953, he has been the lone wolf of the racing industry. He refuses to drive big cars anywhere but Indianapolis. Promoters, who always have cashed in by exploiting the 500-mile champion on the national dirt-track circuit, can't pry Vukie out of Fresno. "I win the big money and I'm satisfied," he says. "The rest of racing they can stick up their radiator."

One four-figure offer after another has been rejected by the man who allegedly "won't do anything for the game that made him rich." He has passed up $2,500 single-race guarantees, $1,000 a week to join a thrill-circus and $2,500 to run the Keck Special around the Chrysler Corporation proving ground. Since last June, Vukie has made but five public appearances. Two were casual midget-auto sprints, mostly for what Vukie considers fun. Another was the Pan-American Road Race. A fourth was for Chrysler. Only when the company raised the ante to $5,000 did Vukie assent. Just once—in the Milwaukee, Wis., 100-mile AAA feature last June—did he wheel a big car. He went 77 miles, found his steering mechanism faulty and pulled off the track.

Then he went home to Fresno. For the next six months, he stayed there.

Such behavior angers promoters who know they could pack in fans if they could advertise Vukovich's name and automobile. While they gripe about him, he lives quietly in Fresno, a grape-and-cotton center of 150,000. There he earns a dollar in a manner that astonishes everyone.

Drive your car up to the gas pump of a small filling station in the downtown area and the man who hastens to clean your windows and check the oil—is Billy

Vukovich! He's proprietor, attendant and toilet-sweeper in one. In a good month he might clear $600 with the station. He works eight hours daily and goes home greasy every night. Parked on the station lot is the swanky yellow-and-black convertible pace car from Indianapolis Speedway. This is the bonus prize awarded the winning driver each year. The interior is of expensive, two-tone leather; the exterior is emblazoned with details of Vukie's

second 500-mile victory.

"It's a kick to see him drive it to work in his grease-monkey's clothes," remarks Fresno mayor Gordon (Slinger) Dunn, the onetime Olympic discus thrower.

Vukovich, who regards the fact that he has two handsome pace cars somewhat diffidently, is at the station from 8:30 to 5:30, six days a week. He'll run up a kid's jalopy on the lubricating hoist and service it as if it were a millionaire rancher's Cadillac. He often works late at night, worrying over profit-and-loss on gallons of gas pumped, where the retail operator's profit is a fraction of a penny per gallon. Owning the three-man station, worth only peanuts compared to what Vukovich could earn by putting himself on countrywide display, is very important to him.

"I'll tell you why," he says. "I've got a wife and two kids." Esther Vukovich, a onetime school classmate of her husband, is one of the prettiest of racing wives. Their children are Bill, Jr., 13, and Marlene, 11. "You can't buy life insurance as a driver and there're more widows than happy old couples in the racket." Vukie goes on. "Esther takes a beating every time I race. She won't say anything, but I know what she goes through."

Most racing wives implore their husbands to give it up. Few succeed. Esther Vukovich has, however, to the point that "Vukie the Hermit" appears far more sparingly than any other name performer today. She married him in 1941, when he was one of the wildest midget drivers on the West Coast. One night at San Diego, he locked wheels with another car, flipped over a ten-foot wall and landed on his head. "I went right over the wall from the grandstand," she tells you. "All Billy had was bruises and a headache." In those days, she sat in the box reserved for wives at tracks. It was a terrible baptism for a young wife.

Wives or girl friends of Swede Lindskog, Ed Haddad, Bill Sheffier, Jim Holt, Clarence Brooks, Bob Rozzano, Tommy Wise, Buck Whitmer, Pinkie Hill, Chick Barbo and Don Ranke were her friends . . . and all saw their men killed in crashes. At times, Esther had to force herself to go to the track. Vukie was overdue for a bad pileup, and everyone knew it.

Strangely, considering the carnage that eventually caused the midgets to lose popularity on the Coast, it never came. Beal Simmons once ran right up Vukovich's tail, climbed his car and sent both cartwheeling into the infield. At Fresno Speedway, Vukie turned another midget into junk after an awesome flip-flop. He got out with only a broken shoulder and wrist and went back to racing with such zeal that he won the 1950 National AAA championship.

When the midget market collapsed in 1951, Vukie moved up in class. But he did so with a caution that surprised everyone. On quarter-mile dromes, a midget can't travel more than 70 mph. Indianapolis-specification power cars, at top speed, cover a two-and-one-half-mile lap in one minute, four seconds, turning the landscape into a grey blur when revved-up to the 180 mph maximum. Engineering of many tracks has fallen far behind advanced speeds, lengthening the odds against survival. Vukie measured this against his family obligations. So he decided to point for the one big purse in the business and never again press his luck.

Vukovich reminds you that it isn't at Indianapolis that drivers are killed. Shorty Catlon, in 1947, was the last fatality during actual 500-mile racing. Most of the accidents that have taken the lives of more than 100 pilots on U.S. tracks since 1950 have come during the grinding, town-hopping, dirt-track tour before and after Memorial Day. "You get tired, or the machine does," Vukie says. "You make one slip, you're gone. They couldn't pay enough money to get me on the circuit."

His critics reply that if Vukie wasn't so remarkably hot on one day a year if he hadn't scaled the top so suddenly—he'd be barnstorming like all the rest. Vukie's rebuttal is: "Nuts."

In 1951, his first 500-miler, he broke down after 29 laps. In 1952, although cracking up on the 191st lap, he won $23,000 in lap and place money ($150 a lap to the pace-setting car). In 1953, he gunned to an upset victory worth a record $89,496. Last year, leading on less laps than in '53, his purse was $74,934. Under his deal with owner Howard Keck, he retains about 40 per cent of all winnings. In three years he's banked about $75,000, plus $15,000 in endorsements and pace cars—which helps explain why he considers the 500-miler a career in itself.

Exceedingly thrifty, probably because he grew up a poor farm boy in Fresno, Vukie intends to expand his business with his winnings. He hopes to own a chain of gas stations. He has plans for a string of quickie carwashes. His older brother, Mike, is a successful garage-owner in Fresno. An expert mechanic, Vukie may enter that field, too. "Most hot-shot drivers wind up broke at 50," he says. "Not this boy. I'm 35 and I give myself only two, three more years on the track. Maybe I'm not popular. But I'm building security."

It's too bad, from the fans' viewpoint, that Vukovich isn't more active. Speedway throttlemen run to dour, colorless personalities, but Vukie stirs excitement every time he gets into a racing car. Although he stands only five-nine and weighs 165, he has big hands and powerful shoulders. One day at Bakersfield, California, an argument broke out between Cal Niday and another driver. Niday's opponent, a 200-pounder, started to take him apart. Niday has only one leg, the result of a crack-up. He stood no chance. "Hang on, Cal! I'm coming!" hollered Vukie, sprinting across the track. Swinging one punch he knocked the big boy over the hood of a car and out.

The kayo wasn't as spectacular, however, as the Vukovich-Al Heath feud, which had Coast racing fans talking for months. Heath, known as the "Blond Bomb" from Seattle, boasted he'd run Vukovich into the grandstand for "shutting the gate" on him. This is the hazardous but effective technique of steering high on the turns to prevent a rival from passing on the outside, then cutting sharply to the rail when he tries to pass on the inside. For 30 laps at Gilmore Stadium in Los Angeles, Vukovich shut the gate on Heath. But the Seattle daredevil had a trick left. He faked an attempt to pass high on the crash rail. When Vukie slid up to block him, Heath cut inside with throttle jammed to the floorboard. Metal screamed as he scraped past Vukie into the lead.

Twenty thousand fans then were treated to a frightening sight. Vukovich, at mile-a-minute speed, began bumping Heath's rear end. Any moment the bumping could send both cars spinning off into a fiery crash. The enraged Vukovich kept slamming Heath while officials frantically signaled with "stop" flags—until Heath gave up. He pulled wide and Vukovich sped on to victory.

"Crazy stuff," he says now. "They almost threw me out of racing for that. Maybe that's why I play it safe today—like a reformed drunkard won't take even a beer."

His early reckless habits are easily understood. Vukie was one of eight children born to hard-pressed Serbian emigrant parents. He grew up in the section of central California described in *Grapes of Wrath* by John Steinbeck. In Fresno, at 14, he was farmed out to a Hindu cotton-grower as a field hand. He might have worked as a crop-laborer all his life but for seeing his first automobile race when he was 16. Without the price of a ticket, he sat on the backstretch fence of the Fresno Fairgrounds. "Floyd Roberts won the main event," he recalls, "and when I saw him blowin' and goin' in a cloud of smoke, I knew I was all through chopping cotton."

His first car was a Model-T which he jazzed up with old motor parts. Then he got a job "stooging" in the pits at the Fairgrounds—pushing roadsters and midgets onto the track, changing tires and oil. At 18, he talked his way behind the wheel of racing roadster. He won $50 third-place money. After that, little Vukie was in Gasoline Alley to stay.

Considered too courageous for his own good, he was regarded as a poor risk by major car owners when he finally set his sights on Indianapolis. In 1950, he went to the 500-miler and braced several people for a ride. They told him to go get a reputation for handling a $50,000 car both speedily and safely. Vukie sat in the stands as one of his Coast ex-midget rivals, Johnny Parsons, won the $53,000 first prize.

Spurned, Vukie had to temporarily return to midgets. The president of Superior Oil Company of Los Angeles, Howard Keck, a wealthy racing buff, saw him win a 100-miler at Pomona. Keck liked his charging, bulldog style of driving which he blended with a deft sense of timing and lightning reactions when in trouble. When he first spoke to Vukie, Keck asked: "If I trust you with my Indianapolis car, will you get it back to me in one piece?" Vukie replied, "Yes, sir. Because I'll be in it." That was the turning point for him.

The No. 14 Fuel Injection Special, built by Kurtis-Kraft of Los Angeles, has a supercharged four-cylinder Offenhauser engine and features a low-slung suspension system which leaves the pilot almost buried in the machine's innards. A low center of gravity gives No. 14 unusual track grip. Fuel is squirted into the cylinders with injectors rather than drawn by suction through a conventional manifold and carburetor, increasing speed. Lightly built—1,750 pounds, about 100 pounds under normal—No. 14 probably is the greatest vehicle ever wheeled out at Indianapolis. It has won twice in three tries. It has led on 436 of the last 600 laps, set an elapsed-time record of three hours, 49 minutes, 17:27 seconds, more than a minute under any other timing in "500" history, and has won $65,900 in lap prizes alone.

Nevertheless, Keck isn't running No. 14 at the Speedway this year. "Already it's obsolete," he says. "We're building a better model at $60,000 cost which will be ready in 1956." For the coming classic, Vukie will pilot a streamlined Kurtis-Kraft owned by Howard Lindsay, a Miami sportsman. How fast it will go hasn't been revealed. But one clue indicating that Vukie may have another record-smasher is that gas consumption of the car is three miles to the gallon. The Blue Crown Specials of Lou Moore, which won at Indianapolis in 1947-48-49 went ten miles per gallon.

Vukie began some unique preparations for his May 30 date in Indianapolis early in March. Because of his stay-at-home policy, he doesn't get wheel-toughened like his competitors. So Vukie trains for Indianapolis like Rocky Marciano prepares for a single big fight a year. "Our place," sighs Esther Vukovich, speaking of the modest, three-bedroom family bungalow in Fresno, "is the only home that's a gymnasium. Vukie does more roadwork than six mailmen."

Leg cramps have caused many 500-mile drivers to fold up in the late stages. On an English racer bicycle, Vukovich bumps 15 miles daily over Fresno's hills and dales. So that his hands won't knot into helpless lumps after fighting a wheel for nearly four hours, he has two exercises—doing 100 fingertip push-ups each day and lifting weights. He skips rope and punches a light bag for endurance. He is a bug on diet, touching nothing that would add an ounce of fat to his 165 pounds.

"Don't kid yourself this isn't an athletic contest, too," insists Vukie, who casts a dim eye at the party-loving, hard-drinking competition. "I don't even smoke because it might cut my wind. When you've been sucking in pulverized rubber dust and oil spray all afternoon, breathing becomes one hell of a problem."

At Indianapolis, Vukie and his wife avoid the Speedway set during the qualifying period. They rent a room in a private home far from the hotel hi-jinks and general hysteria that hits the city at holiday time. The day of the race, Vukie gets up after ten hours of sleep. He has a big breakfast at 6:30, gets to the Speedway by 8 a.m. and runs a personal check on his car.

"My mechanics—Jim Travers and Frank Coon—are the world's best. But I like to listen to that baby myself a long time before taking off." Last year, the Keck Special motor was given seven overhauls before Vukovich was satisfied.

When the starting bomb explodes, Vukie's tactic is to get well up front as soon as possible—away from possible pileups, with room to maneuver. Poor qualifying runs put him in 19th place—the seventh row—at the 1954 start. Yet after only seven laps he'd moved to eighth place; by 39 laps he was fourth; at 71 laps he buzzed past Art Cross and Jimmy Daywalt into the lead.

What's it like during the grind? "Like standing on the Hollywood freeway at 5 p.m. and ducking traffic," he says. "There's no fun in it at those speeds, no thrill. It's all concentration. The first 100 miles aren't so tough. After that you have to fight to stay alert. Your eyes water, you ache all over, your head pounds and you're dying for a drink. But you never can stop thinking."

Watching 32 other cars, handling your own wagon,

keeping an eye on your tachometer and pressure gauge, your pit crew for signals, the position board on the grandstand pagoda which tells you where you stand each lap, signal lights and watching for signs of tire wear require a coordination of body and brain which no other sport equals.

One reason he picks himself to win a third straight time on Memorial Day is that mechanics Travers and Coon will be with him again. Either can change a tire in ten seconds flat. On the 62nd lap last year, Vukie needed fuel and a two-tire change. He'd scarcely braked when Travers and Coon had his car on jacks. He wiped his face, had a drink of cold (not ice) water, adjusted his safety belt—and got the signal to roll. Time: 46 seconds. Two pit stops by Vukie consumed one minute, 42 seconds. Runner-up Jimmy Bryan took 2:04 in the pits—and Bryan lost to Vukovich by exactly one lap. "Even if Bryan had been gaining on me at the end, which he sureinhell wasn't, he couldn't have made up that 18-second edge my crew gave me," Vukie says.

How about the critics who won't yet concede his greatness? "This year might do it," says Vukie. "If I win, they won't have much argument left will they?"

Technically, no. But by winning, he won't—and doesn't expect to—gain in popularity with the bosses of commercialized racing. Before the bricks are cold at Indianapolis, Vukie will be gone. Gone home, to his kids, his home, his gas pump—and he fully intends, to a long, full, normal life.

VUKOVICH'S WRECK

One "Sport" We Can Do Without

TIME OUT WITH THE EDITORS
SEPTEMBER 1955

We didn't say anything about it while we were still rocked by the first wave of shock and revulsion; we wanted to have time to gain a little perspective on the thing. But it's time now to say what we think about the Indianapolis 500 automobile race—and what we think is that it ought to be abolished.

There is no room in this country for a so-called sports event that lasts only a few hours one day a year and yet has produced 46 dead men in its 46-year history.

People have been unhappy about the race for years. Every time it has claimed another victim in one of those gruesome smash-ups, feeling against the event has increased. But when two men were offered as sacrificial victims to the Great God Speed this spring, Manuel Ayulo dying in a trial run two weeks before the race and two-time champion Bill Vukovich giving up his life on the big day, public reaction was sharper than ever before.

There's no sense beating around the bush about it. Most of those who think the race ought to be stopped, and this includes us, feel that it's a Roman-holiday type of spectacle that relies for its appeal upon the morbid desire of some thrill-seekers to watch other, braver men gamble their flesh and blood in a revolving meat grinder that sometimes allows them to pass through safely—and sometimes doesn't. We don't think anywhere near 150,000 people would flock to the Indianapolis track if past performances didn't make it practically a sure thing that somebody would die in a flaming wreck, and others narrowly escape with their lives, before the race had run its course.

This is sport? Not by us, it isn't.

There is more than sketchy evidence that Bill Vukovich didn't think much of it, either, which is why a lot of auto-racing nuts took a dim view of Bill's attitude before his elevation to the roll of gold-star drivers made it downright immoral to belittle his devotion to the "sport." Vukovich, as he made clear to our man Al Stump when Al interviewed him for *SPORT* a couple of months before the race that claimed his life, wasn't very optimistic about a race-driver's chances of living to a ripe old age. He refused point-blank to join "the circuit" and race the year 'round. "You make one slip, you're gone," he said succinctly.

He wasn't kidding.

As everybody knows, the justification for the slaughter at Indianapolis Speedway is that the track serves as a proving ground for the automobiles all of us drive. There may be some slight merit to this argument but we doubt it. For one thing, our automobile manufacturers are way past the experimental stage. They no longer require daredevil drivers to make death-defying tests of their products in order to insure that the things will work. And in the second place, the hope of its builders that Indianapolis would be used as a proving ground by the car industry was torpedoed years ago. All the companies have their own test areas. They neither need nor want Indianapolis.

There's nothing to be gained by avoiding the facts. The race is held because it's a profitable proposition. It attracts a whopping crowd every Memorial Day because there are a lot of people who get a kick out of seeing men risk death—and even, much as we hate to admit it, a lot of people who will go way out of their way to see a gruesome accident happen. If it were possible for such a race to be run off for years on end without anybody being killed or badly hurt, the chances are the crowds would begin to slip noticeably. It isn't pretty but that's the way it is. Nor is it just the famous 500 that depends upon sudden death for its appeal; all auto-racing is the same. How many times have you heard somebody tell about seeing a sensational crack-up in a race? Now, tell the truth; didn't he talk about it with an awed excitement, with the attitude that, boy, he was lucky to have been in on it?

That's why we're against it. We can't see how anybody benefits from such depraved, pagan pandering to the most morbid craving a human being can have. True, nobody forces the drivers to enter. But wave enough money at a hungry man and he'll be tempted to try any fool thing. The instinct is there. But that doesn't mean we have to cater to it.

Epilogue

Fifty years later, most of the heroes of those mystical summer and fall afternoons and winter evenings of 1955 have left us. The Dodgers quit Brooklyn for the glitter of Los Angeles in 1958. Rocky Marciano never did make the comeback so many expected, lived comfortably in retirement but died far too young, on the eve of his 46th birthday in a plane crash in 1969. Sugar Ray Robinson made several comebacks, retired for good at 44 in 1965 and dabbled in acting before his health began to deteriorate; he passed away due to complications from Alzheimer's at 67 in 1989. Mickey Mantle and Eddie Mathews each hit 500 home runs but age, injuries and lifestyle caught up to both of them about the same time. The last season for each was 1968, and both died relatively young, Mantle at 63 of cancer in 1995 and Mathews of complications from pneumonia at 69 in 2001, a few years after an accident on a Caribbean cruise that sapped his strength and spirit. Pancho Gonzalez, 67 and a fireball to the end, was felled by cancer in 1995. Doak Walker, who married former Olympic skier Skeeter Werner after football and moved to Colorado, crashed during a downhill run at Steamboat Springs in 1998. Paralyzed, he fought gamely but passed away from complications a few months later at 71. A very fit and seemingly healthy Wilt Chamberlain took his leave suddenly, the victim of heart failure at 63 in 1999. Maurice Richard waged a long battle with abdominal cancer before succumbing at age 78 in 2000.

Willie Mays, Bill Russell, Jean Beliveau and Arnold Palmer are all in their 70s now, but the shadows cast by their legends have only grown larger with the passage of the years, with each now reigning as the ultimate living icon of his sport.

Appendix

Standings, Champions, Award Winners

AUTO RACING

NASCAR season champion: Tim Flock
AAA Racing season champion: Bob Sweikert
Indianapolis 500: Bob Sweikert
Formula One championship: Juan Manuel Fangio
24 Hours of LeMans: Mike Hawthorn / Ivor Bueb (Jaguar).
Notable: Attempting to become the first winner of three consecutive Indy 500s, Bill Vukovich, 36, is killed in a five-car crash ... The 24 Hours of LeMans is marred by a multi-car collision that results in 80 deaths when cars careen into the grandstand.

BASEBALL

NATIONAL LEAGUE

	W	L	Pct.	GB
Brooklyn	98	55	.641	—
Milwaukee	85	69	.552	13.5
New York	80	74	.519	18.5
Philadelphia	77	77	.500	21.5
Cincinnati	75	79	.487	23.5
Chicago	72	81	.471	26
St. Louis	68	86	.442	30.5
Pittsburgh	60	94	.390	38.5

MVP: Roy Campanella, BRO
Rookie: Bill Virdon, STL
Batting: Richie Asburn, PHI, .338
Home Runs: Willie Mays, NY, 51
RBIs: Duke Snider, BRO, 136

Wins: Robin Roberts, PHI, 23

ERA: Bob Friend, PIT, 2.83
Strikeouts: Sam Jones, CHI, 198

AMERICAN LEAGUE

	W	L	Pct.	GB
New York	96	58	.623	—
Cleveland	93	61	.604	3
Chicago	91	63	.591	5
Boston	84	70	.545	12
Detroit	79	75	.513	17
Kansas City	63	91	.409	33
Baltimore	57	97	.370	39
Washington	53	101	.344	43

MVP: Yogi Berra, NY
Rookie: Herb Score, CLE
Batting: Al Kaline, DET, .340
Home Runs: Mickey Mantle, NY, 37
RBIs: Jackie Jensen, BOS;
    Ray Boone, DET, 116
Wins: Frank Sullivan, BOS; Whitey
    Ford, NY; Bob Lemon, CLE, 18
ERA: Billy Pierce, CHI, 1.97
Strikeouts: Herb Score, CLE, 245

WORLD SERIES
Brooklyn Dodgers 4, New York Yankees 3
Sep. 28: New York 6, Brooklyn 5
Sep. 29: New York 4, Brooklyn 2
Sep. 30: Brooklyn 8, New York 3
Oct. 1: Brooklyn 8, New York 5
Oct. 2: Brooklyn 5, New York 3
Oct. 3: New York 5, Brooklyn 1
Oct. 4: Brooklyn 2, New York 0
MVP: Johnny Podres, BRO

Notable: The Kansas City Athletics, formerly the Philadelphia Athletics, win just 63 games in their first season ... When Johnny Podres shuts out the Yankees 2-0 in Game 7, the Dodgers win their first World Series in eight attempts ... Phillies pitcher Robin Roberts records his sixth-consecutive season of at least 20 wins ... Ernie Banks sets a major-league record with five grand slams in one season ... Willie Mays becomes the seventh player to hit 50 home runs in a season ... Al Kaline, 20, becomes the youngest batting champion in history when he takes the AL crown.

BASKETBALL

NATIONAL BASKETBALL ASSOCIATION
1954-55 STANDINGS

Eastern Division

	W	L	Pct.	GB
Syracuse	43	29	.597	—
New York	38	34	.528	5
Boston	36	36	.500	7
Philadelphia	33	39	.458	10
Baltimore *	3	11	.214	—

* Baltimore folded November 27, 1954

Western Division

	W	L	Pct.	GB
Fort Wayne	43	29	.597	—
Minneapolis	40	32	.556	3
Rochester	29	43	.403	14
Milwaukee	26	46	.361	17

Top Rookie: Bob Pettit, MIL
Scoring Leader: Neil Johnston, PHI, 22.7
Field Goal Leader: Larry Foust, FW, .487
Free Throw Leader: Bill Sharman, BOS, .897
Assist Leader: Bob Cousy, BOS, 7.9
Rebound Leader: Neil Johnston, PHI, 15.1

Notable: In the first season of the 24-second clock, scoring jumps by 14 points per game ... With a 3-11 record in late November, the Baltimore Bullets go bankrupt and drop out of the league ... On Dec. 15, Minneapolis and Seattle combine to set a league record by scoring 268 points in a game, won by Syracuse, 135-133, in triple OT ... Bill Sharman hits for 55 consecutive free throws, setting a record that stands for 19 years ... The 1955-56 season sees the first NBA all-star game.

FINALS
Syracuse 4, Fort Wayne 3
Mar. 31: Fort Wayne 82 at Syracuse 86
Apr. 2: Fort Wayne 84 at Syracuse 87
Apr. 3: Syracuse 89, Fort Wayne (at Indianapolis) 96
Apr. 5: Syracuse 102, Fort Wayne (at Indianapolis) 109
Apr. 7: Syracuse 71, Fort Wayne (at Indianapolis) 74
Apr. 9: Fort Wayne 104 at Syracuse 109
Apr. 10: Fort Wayne 91 at Syracuse 92

1955-56 STANDINGS

Eastern Division

	W	L	Pct.	GB
Philadelphia	45	27	.625	—
Boston	39	33	.542	6
Syracuse	35	37	.486	10
New York	35	37	.486	10

Western Division

	W	L	Pct.	GB
Fort Wayne	37	35	.514	—
Minneapolis	33	39	.458	4
St. Louis	33	39	.458	4
Rochester	31	41	.431	6

MVP: Bob Pettit, STL
Top Rookie: Maurice Stokes, ROC
Scoring Leader: Bob Pettit, STL, 25.7
Field Goal Leader: Neil Johnston, PHI, .457
Free Throw Leader: Bill Sharman, BOS, .867
Assist Leader: Bob Cousy, BOS, 8.9
Rebound Leader: Bob Pettit, STL, 16.2

FINALS

Philadelphia 4, Fort Wayne 1

Mar. 31: Fort Wayne 94 at Philadelphia 98
Apr. 1: Philadelphia 83 at Fort Wayne 84
Apr. 3: Fort Wayne 96 at Philadelphia 100
Apr. 5: Philadelphia 107 at Fort Wayne 105
Apr. 7: Fort Wayne 88 at Philadelphia 99

NCAA

Championship: San Francisco 77, La Salle 63
Third Place: Colorado 75, Iowa 74
Semifinals: La Salle 76, Iowa 73; San Francisco 62, Colorado 50
Tournament MVP: Bill Russell, San Francisco
Notable: Bill Russell has 23 points, 25 rebounds in final, as teammate K.C. Jones scores 24 while holding La Salle's Tom Gola to 16.

National Invitational Tournament

Championship: Duquesne 70, Dayton 58
Tournament MVP: Maurice Stokes, St. Francis, PA
Notable: Duquesne's Sihugo Green scores 33 points in final.

BOXING

Ring Magazine Fighter of the Year: Rocky Marciano (KOs vs. Ezzard Charles and Archie Moore to retain Heavyweight belt)
Ring Magazine Fight of the Year: Carmen Basilio KO 12th round vs. Tony DeMarco
Champions
Flyweight: Pascual Perez, Argentina
Bantamweight: Robert Cohen, France
Featherweight: Sandy Saddler, USA
Lightweight: James Carter, USA; Wallace (Bud) Smith, USA (Smith 15-round decision vs. Carter, May 29, Boston)
Welterweight: Johnny Saxton, USA; Tony DeMarco, USA; Carmen Basilio, USA (DeMarco KO 15th round vs. Saxton, April 1, Boston; Basilio KO 12th round vs. DeMarco, May 10, Syracuse)
Middleweight: Carl (Bobo) Olson, USA; Sugar Ray Robinson, USA (Robinson KO 2nd round vs. Olson, Dec. 9, Chicago)

Light Heavyweight: Archie Moore, USA
Heavyweight: Rocky Marciano, USA
Notable: Marciano's KO of Archie Moore is his last fight. He retires as undefeated champion (49-0) ... Sugar Ray Robinson regains the title following a two-year retirement ... Floyd Patterson, 19, defeats Joe Gannon for his first pro victory.

CYCLING

Tour de France: Louison Bobet, France (three-time winner)
World Cycling championship: Stan Ockers, Belgium

FOOTBALL

NATIONAL FOOTBALL LEAGUE

East	W	L	T	West	W	L	T
Cleveland Browns	9	2	1	Los Angeles Rams	8	3	1
Washington Redskins	8	4	0	Chicago Bears	8	4	0
New York Giants	6	5	1	Green Bay Packers	6	6	0
Philadelphia Eagles	4	7	1	Baltimore Colts	5	6	1
Chicago Cardinals	4	7	1	San Francisco 49ers	4	8	0
Pittsburgh Steelers	4	8	0	Detroit Lions	3	9	0

Championship: Cleveland Browns 38, Los Angeles Rams 14
All-Star Game: All-Stars 30, Cleveland 27 (attendance: 75,000)
MVP: Otto Graham, Cleveland
Rookie of the Year: Alan Ameche, Baltimore
Scoring Leader: Doak Walker, Detroit, 128 points
Rushing Leader: Alan Ameche, Baltimore, 961 yards
Passing Leader: Otto Graham, Cleveland, 98 of 185, 1721 yards, 11 TDs
Receiving Leader: Pete Pihos, Philadelphia, 63, 864 yards, 13.9 avg., 7 TDs
Notable: After being cut by Pittsburgh, free agent Johnny Unitas is signed by the Baltimore Colts ... Otto Graham comes out of retirement early in the season and quarterbacks Cleveland to the NFL championship, passing for 209 yards and scoring 2 TDs in his final game, as his Los Angeles counterpart, Norm Van Brocklin throws six interceptions.

CANADIAN FOOTBALL LEAGUE
Grey Cup: Edmonton Eskimos 34, Montreal Alouettes 19
Outstanding Player: Pat Abbruzzi, Montreal

NCAA
Champion: Oklahoma (11-0-0)
Heisman Memorial Trophy: Howard Cassady, Ohio State
Rose Bowl: Ohio State 20, Southern California 7
Orange Bowl: Duke 34, Nebraska 7
Sugar Bowl: Navy 21, Mississippi 0
Cotton Bowl: Georgia Tech 14, Arkansas 6
Sun Bowl: UTEP 47, Florida State 20
Gator Bowl: Auburn 33, Baylor 13
Citrus Bowl: Northeast-Omaha 7, Eastern Kentucky 6

GOLF

MEN

Masters: Cary Middlecoff   **US Open:** Jack Fleck
British Open: Peter Thomson   **PGA Championship:** Doug Ford
Ryder Cup: United States 8, Great Britain 4
Walker Cup: United States 10, Great Britain/Ireland 2
PGA Player of the Year: Doug Ford
PGA money leader: Julius Boros, $63,122
PGA scoring leader: Sam Snead, 69.86
Notable: Mike Souchak, with a record 27 on the back nine, shoots 60 in the first round of the Texas Open and wins with a record-low total of 257 ... Arnold Palmer wins the Canadian Open for his first pro victory ... Jack Fleck scores one of the biggest upsets in golf history by defeating Ben Hogan in a playoff at the US Open.

WOMEN

US Women's Open: Fay Crocker   **LPGA Championship:** Beverly Hanson
LPGA money leader: Patty Berg, $16,492
LPGA scoring leader: Patty Berg, 74.47

HOCKEY

NATIONAL HOCKEY LEAGUE

1954-55 STANDINGS

Team	GP	W	L	T	Pts
Detroit	70	42	17	11	95
Montreal	70	41	18	11	93
Toronto	70	24	24	22	70
Boston	70	23	26	21	67
New York	70	17	35	18	52
Chicago	70	13	40	17	43

AWARDS

Hart: Ted Kennedy, TOR
Art Ross: Bernie Geoffrion, MTL
Vezina: Terry Sawchuk, DET
Norris: Doug Harvey, MTL
Calder: Ed Litzenberger, CHI

STANLEY CUP FINALS

Detroit 4, Montreal 3

Apr 3: Montreal 2 at Detroit 2
Apr 5: Montreal 1 at Detroit 7
Apr 7: Detroit 2 at Montreal 4
Apr 9: Detroit 3 at Montreal 5
Apr 10: Montreal 1 at Detroit 5
Apr 12: Detroit 3 at Montreal 6
Apr 14: Montreal 1 at Detroit 3

1955-56 STANDINGS

Team	GP	W	L	T	Pts
Montreal	70	45	15	10	100
Detroit	70	30	24	16	76
New York	70	32	28	10	74
Toronto	70	24	33	13	61
Boston	70	23	34	13	59
Chicago	70	19	39	12	50

AWARDS

Hart: Jean Beliveau, MTL
Art Ross: Jean Beliveau, MTL
Vezina: Jacques Plante, MTL
Norris: Doug Harvey, MTL
Calder: Glenn Hall, DET

STANLEY CUP FINALS

Montreal 4, Detroit 1

Mar 31: Detroit 4 at Montreal 6
Apr 3: Detroit 1 at Montreal 5
Apr 5: Montreal 1 at Detroit 3
Apr 8: Montreal 3 at Detroit 0
Apr 10: Detroit 1 at Montreal 3

World Championship: Canada (Penticton Bees) 5, USSR 0
Notable: For the first time in history, hockey appears on the front page of *The New York Times* following a riot in Montreal on March 17 after Canadiens' star Maurice Richard was suspended for the season ... Gordie Howe, with 20 points in 11 playoff games (9 goals, 11 assists), including 12 points in the 1955 final (5 goals, 7 assists) sets two playoff scoring records.

HORSE RACING

Kentucky Derby: Swaps, Willie Shoemaker
Preakness Stakes: Nashua, Eddie Arcaro
Belmont Stakes: Nashua, Eddie Arcaro

Notable: Nashua, trained by "Sunny" Jim Fitzsimmons, is named three-year-old colt of the year after defeating Swaps in one of the most famous match races in thoroughbred history. Held at Chicago's Washington Park, Nashua won the $100,000 winner-takes-all race by six lengths, handing Swaps its only loss in nine outings as a three-year-old.

SKATING

World Figure Skating Championships
Men's champion: Hayes Alan Jenkins, USA
Women's champion: Tenley Albright, USA
Pairs champions: Frances Dafoe & Norris Bowden, Canada

TENNIS

MEN
Australian Championship:
   Ken Rosewall
French Championships:
   Tony Trabert
Wimbledon: Tony Trabert
US Championships: Tony Trabert
Davis Cup: Australia 5, U.S. 0

WOMEN
Australian Championship:
   Beryl Penrose
French Championships:
   Angela Mortimer
Wimbledon: Louise Brough
US Championships: Doris Hart
Wightman Cup: U.S. 6, Great Britain 1

Notable: Maureen Connolly, winner of 9 major championships, retires due to injuries sustained in a 1954 horseback-riding accident ... Tony Trabert's Grand Slam bid is thwarted by a semi-final loss to Ken Rosewall at the Australian Open ... The No. 1 year-end rankings are claimed by Trabert and Louise Brough.

Photo & Illustration Credits